HOW THEY TRAIN: HIGH SCHOOL FIELD EVENTS

by Frank P. Calore

TAFNEWS PRESS
Book Division of Track & Field News

Production Staff: Grace Light

Jacket Design: Ann Harris.

Library of Congress Catalog Card Number: 80-50278.
Standard Book Number: 0-911520-95-3.

Printed in the United States of America.

Photo Credits

PHOTO OF:	BY:
Sally McCarthy	Oklahoma University
Steve Moore	Chambersburg *Trojan*
Bob Smith	Roy Atkins
Jeff Buckingham	John Burke
Joe Dial	Rich Clarkson
Greg Duplantis	John Boss/*Capital City Press*
Bill Lange	David Zinman
Eric Richard	Jeff Johnson
David Hintz	Milwaukee Public Schools
Carl Lewis	Don Chadez
Keith Richardson	Bryan Sta. High School
Michael Carter	Don Chadez
Dan Krueger	Mark Mitchell
Dana Olson	Brad Caldwell
Elaine Sobansky	Carol Myers
Cindy Browning	White River High School
Carol Lewis	Dave Cuskey
Ken Riedl	Cheyenne Central High School

Cover photo of Clint Johnson by John Burke

Table of Contents

Introduction 4
HIGH JUMP 5
Dianne Depp 6
Granville Hayes, Jr. 8
Michael Jacob 10
Josh King 12
Sally McCarthy 15
Steve Moore 17
Michael Nelson 20
Dan Rohrs 22
Bob Smith 24
Peggy Stewart 27
Kenneth Storey 30
Reginald Towns 32

POLE VAULT 35
Paul Brattlof 36
Jeff Buckingham 38
Joe Dial 40
Greg Duplantis 42
Greg Ernst 45
Bubba Kavanaugh 48
Mark Klee 50
Bill Lange 52
Tim McIntyre 54
Mike Mullins 56
Eric Richard 58
LONG JUMP/TRIPLE JUMP 61
Donnie Butler 62
Ken Fowler 64
David Hintz 66
Ricky Holliday 68
Willie Houston 70
Andre Kirnes 72
Carl Lewis 74
Ernest Marvin 77
Keith Richardson 79
Mike Scudieri 81
Darryl Smith 84
Ward Wilson 86
SHOT PUT/DISCUS THROW 88
Michael Carter 89
Danny Flatt 91
Melanie Heitman 93
Jackie Henry 97
Clint Johnson 100
Dan Krueger 102
Dana Olson 105
Peter Pallozzi 108
George Saah 110
George Scribellito 113
Mike Shill 115
Elaine Sobansky 118
Philip Wells 120
Doug Woolen 122
JAVELIN THROW 125
Gray Barrow 126
Tracy Beckes 128
Cindy Browning 130
Brian Cullinan 132
ALL-AROUNDERS 134
Tonya Alston 135
Darnell Johnson 137
Bill Kuntz 139
Paul Lacassagne 141
Carol Lewis 143
John McIntosh 146
Steve Pace 148
Ken Riedl 151
Anna Marie Solomonson 154
Carina Westover 157
Warren Wilhoite 159
About the Author . . . . Back inside cover

Introduction

Every coach has attended clinics to listen and take notes on training techniques and competitive methods. After the organized sessions, we all sit around talking, and the sharp ones will engage in some detailed "brain-picking."

"What's your kid lifting?" "What height's he working out at?" we ask, stealing a workout here, a drill there. Researching is the proper term, and we all do it.

This book is an attempt to research and "brain-pick" the top athletes; to ask them "What are you doing to get so good?" Some answers became quite obvious as I read the material from each athlete. All of these competitors are outstanding all-around athletes, possessing skills that span several areas of speed, strength, and agility. They also show a great deal of dedication to track and field, often giving up other sports to concentrate 100% on their specialty. Every coach dreams of having athletes of this caliber, for both their athletic skills as well as the leadership by example that they extend over a team.

This book is not a guarantee of success in track and field, but rather samples and examples for workouts, allowing coaches and athletes to pick and choose, combine and alter, in order to best design a program that meets their needs to the fullest. Wherever possible (Psyching Up, Training Comments), I have used the athletes' own words, because they can best explain why and how they have reached success. I hope they can transfer their accumulated knowledge as well as their dedication and commitment to the sport to others who work for success in track and field.

A special thanks to everyone, especially the athletes, who helped produce this book. Good luck to all of you.

Frank P. Calore

HIGH JUMP

Dianne Depp

DIANNE DEPP	Owensboro High School
Born 11/8/62	Owensboro, Kentucky
6-0 148	Coaches Jury & Reed

COMPETITIVE HISTORY

Dianne first became interested in cross-country and distance running. Spring track introduced her to the high jump.

BEST MARKS
5-8

AGE GROUP MARKS

Year	Age	HJ
1978	15	5-4½
1979	16	5-8

PREPARING FOR COMPETITION

"Before I jump, I picture myself going over the bar. I try to really concentrate on my present weaknesses. I say to myself that I can't let this person beat me."

TRAINING COMMENTS

"I think cross country has helped strengthen my legs more than anything, and basketball has helped get more

6

spring in my legs." Dianne does not do a great deal of jumping work, but does work on flexibility every day. She uses a 33-foot approach, 14-5 over from her take-off point, starting her curve 13-0 from the bar.

WEIGHT TRAINING PROGRAM
None

DAILY SEASONAL WORKOUTS
Fall
Cross-Country
Winter
Basketball
Spring
Monday—440 warm-up, 4 X 440, 4 X 220, 4 X 110, jog 440
Tuesday—Technique work, form jumping
Wednesday—440 warm-up, 3 X 440, 3 X 220, 3 X 110, jog 440
Thursday—Technique work, form jumping
Friday—Rest
Saturday—Competition
Sunday—Rest
Summer
Some distance running

Granville Hayes, Jr.

GRANVILLE HAYES JR.   Moberly Senior High School

Born 2/10/61   Moberly, Missouri

5-10 155   Coach Ken Ausbury

COMPETITIVE HISTORY

Granville began running in a local AAU summer program at age ten. He competed on the interscholastic level through junior and senior high school, winning the conference, district, and state high jump championships.

BEST MARKS
6-9

AGE GROUP MARKS

Year	Age	HJ	100
1973	12	4-6	—
1974	13	4-8	—
1975	14	5-4	11.6
1976	15	6-0	10.9
1977	16	6-4	10.4
1978	17	6-8	10.5
1979	18	6-9	

PREPARING FOR COMPETITION
"Reading a scripture from the Bible, saying a prayer,

then getting off to myself and concentrating on the competition.

TRAINING COMMENTS

"I don't have specific high jump training exercises. I concentrate on keeping in top shape. I do practice especially hard on getting my approach and take off down. My approach has 9 to 11 steps in a slanted J shape."

WEIGHT TRAINING PROGRAM

Granville lifts weights three days each week during the winter season.

Bench Press	1 X 10 repetitions—light
	4 X 6 repetitions—heavy
Leg Machine	4 X 10 repetitions—heavy
Squats	1 X 10 repetitions—light
	4 X 6 repetitions—heavy

DAILY SEASONAL WORKOUTS

Fall
Football

Winter
Monday—Stretch, run, weight training program, handball

Tuesday—Stretch, run, work on approach, handball

Wednesday—Stretch, run, weight training program, handball

Thursday—Stretch, run, work on approach, handball

Friday—Stretch, run, weight training program, handball

Spring
Everyday—stretch, run, work on approach and form jumping

Summer
Granville runs 3 miles each day and works out to stay in shape for summer meets.

Michael Jacob

MICHAEL M. JACOB   Croton-Harmon High School

Born 11/9/60   Croton, New York

6-4 180   Coach Michael Doehring

COMPETITIVE HISTORY
Mike started out as a sprinter in junior high, switching to the high jump in the 9th grade.

BEST MARKS
6-10½

AGE GROUP MARKS

Year	Age	HJ
1975	14	5-10
1976	15	6-2
1977	16	6-6
1978	17	6-10½

PREPARING FOR COMPETITION
"About 3 hours before competition, I like to lie down and rest. This also gives me time to think of the job I have to do to win the event."

TRAINING COMMENTS

Jacob feels that a good mixture of distance and sprint workouts have been the biggest help in his jumping preparedness.

WEIGHT TRAINING PROGRAM

Mike lifts weights one day a week, winter and spring, doing 3 sets of 10, quarter squats with 130 pounds. He also works out on a jumping machine.

DAILY SEASONAL WORKOUTS
Fall
No training
Winter and Spring
Monday—(440-330-220-110) X 3, weight training program
Tuesday—6-8 miles hard
Wednesday—(440-330-220-110) X 3
Thursday—4-5 miles easy
Friday—Jog 3-4 miles
Saturday—Competition
Sunday—Rest
> Jumping technique practice took place after running workouts
Summer
Mike works out with one day of sprint training and three days of distance running each week.

Josh King

JOSH KING   Skyline High School

Born 6/19/61   Salt Lake City, Utah

6-4   170   Coach R. Craig Poole

COMPETITIVE HISTORY

Josh went out for track because it was the only sport where he could beat his brother and friends. In six years of jumping, King has beaten a great many people as he has won District, Region and State Championships.

BEST MARKS

6-11½

AGE GROUP MARKS

Year	Age	HJ
1974	12	5-3
1975	13	5-8
1976	14	6-2
1977	15	6-9
1978	16	6-10
1979	17	6-11¼

PREPARING FOR COMPETITION

"I do what is called 'sitting in my corner.' I select a very quiet place where I know I won't be interrupted, then relax and carefully go step-by-step over my technique; then I just think about getting off the ground and making it over the bar."

TRAINING COMMENTS
Weight training, running and jumping work are all important. Josh starts his approach 64-0 back and 18-6 over from the pit, taking 3 walking and 11 running steps.

WEIGHT TRAINING PROGRAM

Three days each week		Five days each week	
Bench press	4 X 5	Leg extensions	4 X 20
Leg press	4 X 5	Leg curls	4 X 20
Arm curls	3 X 10	"Leaper"	4 X 35
Dips	2 X 10	Reverse sit-ups	1 X 20

DAILY SEASONAL WORKOUTS
Fall
Monday—Weight training program, stretch, 8 X 110 uphill

Tuesday—Run 2-3 miles, 4-6 X 440 uphill

Wednesday—Weight training program, stretch, easy running

Thursday—Run 2-3 miles, 4-6 X 440 uphill

Friday—Weight training program, stretch, easy running

Saturday—Rest

Sunday—Rest

Winter
Everyday—Basic 8 workout-pushups, "prayers" run, back hyper, hip hyper, toe hooks, leg squeeze, bouncing 5 X 10

Monday—Stretch, basic 8, intervals (110-660), weight training program—jumping practice at night

Tuesday—Stretch, basic 8, light running, depth jumps

Wednesday—Stretch, basic 8, intervals (110-660), weight training program—jumping practice

Thursday—Stretch, basic 8, medium interval workout

Friday—Stretch, basic 8, intervals, weight training program—jumping practice

Saturday—Rest

Sunday—Rest

Spring

>Monday—Stretch, basic 8, jumping practice, weight training program
>
>Tuesday—Stretch, basic 8, jumping practice, depth jumps
>
>Wednesday—Stretch, basic 8, jump for height, weight training program
>
>Thursday—Stretch, basic 8, warm down
>
>Friday—Stretch, basic 8, warm down
>
>Saturday—Compete
>
>Sunday—Rest

Summer

Josh works out three days each week and competes once a week during the summer.

Sally McCarthy

SALLY McCARTHY

Born 5/25/61

5-8   128

Medical Lake High School

Medical Lake, Washington

Coach George Lang

COMPETITIVE HISTORY
The Washington State high jump champion and U.S. Juniors medal winner, Sally began as an eleven-year-old in a Spokane A.A.U. program.

BEST MARKS
5-10   16-4

AGE GROUP MARKS

Year	Age	HJ
1973	12	4-7
1974	13	5-3
1975	14	5-6
1976	15	5-8
1977	16	5-9½
1978	17	5-10
1979	18	5-10

PREPARING FOR COMPETITION

"I have to be by myself and can't let myself watch the competition either warming up or competing."

TRAINING COMMENTS

Sally feels her weight training and running program have been the most important part of her training. She uses a 9-11 step "J" approach, accelerating through a moderate curve to reduce ankle stress.

WEIGHT TRAINING PROGRAM

Sally uses two weight workouts, one concentrating on endurance, the other on heavy, short, strength pressing.

DAILY SEASONAL WORKOUTS

Fall
Volleyball

Weight training program one day each week, endurance program working on spring

Winter
Basketball

Weight training program one day each week, using squats to improve spring

Spring
Monday—Track running (440's, 220's), hurdle work

Tuesday—Weight training—short, heavy, strength program

Wednesday—Light sprinting, starts, jogging

Thursday—Competition

Friday—Distance run, run bleachers

Saturday—Weight training—heavy endurance program

Sunday—Rest

Jumping technique work takes place after running workouts

Summer
Monday—Jog

Tuesday—Sprint workout, jump technique work, weight training program

Thursday—Easy stride work, light jumping

Saturday—Competition

Steve Moore

STEVEN MOORE   Chambersburg Area Senior High School

Born 11/1/61   Chambersburg, Pennsylvania

6-5   182   Coaches Clarence Snart and Richard Nye

COMPETITIVE HISTORY
Steve began his jumping in elementary school in Texas, then moved to Germany where he gained valuable international experience. After returning to the U.S., he won the Navel Academy Invitational, State Championship and U.S.T.F.F. National Age Group Championship.

BEST MARKS
7-1

AGE GROUP MARKS

Year	Age	HJ
1976	14	5-6
1977	15	6-2
1978	16	6-10
1979	17	7-1

PREPARING FOR COMPETITION
"I tend to watch the others jump and then see who will be my competition, then warm-up and jump. I try to psych myself up by trying to relax as much as possible."

TRAINING COMMENTS

Speed training has been the important part of Steve's workouts. He uses a 58-0 approach, 13-6 out from the standard, running the approach in 3.4 seconds.

WEIGHT TRAINING PROGRAM

In the fall, Steve lifts three days a week, working at 70% of maximum until he feels ready to move to 80% about 3 or 4 weeks before the start of the winter season. Weight training is reduced during the competitive season.

Bench Press	Leg Extensions
Leg Press	Squats
Shoulder Press	Inclined Sit-ups
Arm Curls	Cleans
Flys	Leg Curls
	Clean & Jerk

All lifts done in 3 sets of 8

DAILY SEASONAL WORKOUTS

Fall
  Monday-Wednesday-Friday
  Warm up ½ mile jog, stretch, run 4-5 miles, run 3 X 110,
    Weight training program
  Tuesday-Thursday

Warm up 1 mile run, interval workout—440's, 330's, 220's, 110's
Saturday-Sunday
Run 2-6 miles easy
Winter
Basketball
Spring
Monday—1-mile warm-up, 10 X 110, 2 X 220, form jumping at low height, triple jump, weight training program

Tuesday—1-mile warm-up, 2 X 330, 2 X 220, 4 X 110, 1 mile warm-down

Wednesday—3-mile run, light weight training program, 4 X 110, approach work, ½-mile warm-down

Thursday—Competition

Friday—Weight training program, ½-mile warm-up, 2 X 330, 2 X 220, 2 X 110, ½-mile warm-down, triple jump work

Saturday—1-mile run, triple jump and high jump work, light weight training program, 1 mile run, 6 X 110, 10 mile bike ride

Sunday—basketball, run distance

Summer
Monday—1-mile warm-up, 4 X 880 (AM)
 1-mile warm-up, 2 X 330, 4 X 220, 2 X 110, 1-mile warm-down, high jump work (PM)

Tuesday—4-mile run, run hills, stretch (AM)
 weight training program, run 6 miles (PM)

Wednesday—2-mile run (AM)
 Competition (PM)

Thursday—2-mile run, weight training program (AM)
 run 2-3 miles (PM)

Friday—2-mile run, weight training program (AM)
 Run 2 miles of hills, run 3 miles easy, 20 X 110 (PM)

Saturday—2-mile run (AM)
 Run sprints (PM)

Sunday—½-mile warm-up, 1 X 330, 2 X 220, ½-mile warm-down (AM)
 weight training program, run 4 miles (PM)

Michael Nelson

MICHAEL K. NELSON   Interlake High School

Born 10/26/61   Bellevue, Washington

6-4   180   Coach Jack Estep

COMPETITIVE HISTORY
Eventually City, Conference, and Washington State champion, Mike began high jumping in elementary school.

BEST MARKS
7-1¼

AGE GROUP MARKS

Year	Age	HJ
1973	11	4-6
1974	12	5-0
1975	13	5-8
1976	14	6-1
1977	15	6-5
1978	16	7-½
1979	17	7-1¼

PREPARING FOR COMPETITION
"Relaxing . . . not speaking much, constantly thinking of what I'm going to do."

TRAINING COMMENTS
Mike feels that distance running and his strength program have been the biggest aid to his high jump progress.

WEIGHT TRAINING PROGRAM
Nelson uses an isometric program to develop leg strength.

DAILY SEASONAL WORKOUTS
Fall
Soccer
Winter
Basketball
Spring
Monday—Run 2-5 miles, sprints, run stairs, weight training program

Tuesday—Run 1-2 miles, high jump technique work, run sprints

Wednesday—Run 1-2 miles, work on alternate events, weight training program

Thursday—Run 1-2 miles, light "fun" workout

Friday—Competition

Saturday—Rest or invitational meet

Sunday—Rest
Summer
Mike runs distance, competes in all-comers meets and participates in basketball and other sports.

Dan Rohrs

DAN ROHRS   Upper Arlington High School

Born 8/1/61   Columbus, Ohio

5-11   165   Coach Randy Pfeiffer

COMPETITIVE HISTORY

Dan was first exposed to track and field as a 4th grader in an AAU program; he began high jumping at age 11. Slowed by injury as a sophomore, he came into his own in 1978. Ohio State long jump runner-up, he was conference, sectional, district, and State high jump champion. Dan was named to the Adidas All-American Team.

BEST MARKS
7-1¼   23-5

AGE GROUP MARKS

Year	Age	HJ	LJ
1973	11	5-2	15-5
1974	12	5-5	16-7
1975	13	5-9	19-6
1976	14	6-4	22-0
1977	15	6-4	20-2(injured)
1978	16	7-1¼	23-5

PREPARING FOR COMPETITION
Dan has no method of psyching up, but rather finds he

has to work at calming down his nervous energy. During meets he says "he talks a lot" but tries not to bother other jumpers. The night before competition, Dan listens to "mellow music" and reads his Bible as a calming and steadying influence.

TRAINING COMMENTS
Dan feels his weight training and sprint work have been the most important part of his training. He feels that running has been especially important in keeping his legs strong and fresh for good jumps late in competition.

WEIGHT TRAINING PROGRAM
Rohrs worked out six days a week on a Nautilus machine. There were three days of extensive leg lifting, two light to intermediate days, and one day of intensive upper body lifting.

DAILY SEASONAL WORKOUTS
Fall Summer
Football workouts
Winter
Run overdistance every day until the weather was warm enough to work on the track
Spring
Pre-practice warm-up—1 mile jog, 30 minute stretching, stride 6 X 100
Monday—12 X 220 (30 sec) 1:30 rest
Tuesday—Competition—Pre-meet warm-up—1 mile run, 1 hour stretching, stride 6 X 100
Wednesday—1 X 440 (70-75 sec), 2 X 330 (50 sec), 4 X 220 (30 sec), 4 X 110 (15 sec)
Thursday—6 X 220 (30 sec), 4 X 330 (50 sec), 2 X 440 (70 sec)
Friday—4 X 330 (50 sec), walk 110 between, 4 X 220 (30 sec), 1:30 rest between
Saturday—Competition
Sunday—Overdistance
During the early season, Dan trains through all meets, taking no days off, working on jumping technique after his running workout. Workouts are aimed at peaking performances for the major late season meets.

Bob Smith

BOB SMITH   Westminster High School

Born 1/30/62   Westminster, Maryland

6-5   175   Coach Jim Shank

COMPETITIVE HISTORY

Bob went out for track to stay in shape for football. His early success convinced him to give up football and concentrate on his jumping.

BEST MARKS
6-8

AGE GROUP MARKS

Year	Age	HJ
1977(i)	15	5-8
1977	15	6-4
1978(i)	16	6-8
1978	16	6-8
1979	17	7-0

PREPARING FOR COMPETITION

"At the meet I watch my competitors practice jumping, stretch and limber up. I try to make my mind a blank when standing ready to jump. I stare at a fixed spot on the bar; that seems to make the bar look lower. People watching seem

to give me confidence, and I try to stay to myself while competing."

TRAINING COMMENTS
   Bob credits his overall training program, weight training, sprint work, and jumping at the bar set at higher than usual height, as the reasons for his success. Also, he reads as much as possible about high jumpers and jumping technique.

WEIGHT TRAINING PROGRAM
   "Keep the weight constant for each lift until you can do all sets comfortably. Then, increase the weight at the next workout."

Bench press	3 X 8
Leg press	5 X 12
Half squats	3 X 12
Deltoid raise	2 X 20
Pulldowns on machine	2 X 20

   40 situps on incline board, increased by 20 each week until 100. On Wednesday, eliminate bench press and deltoid raise, add curls 3 X 12 and military press 3 X 12.

DAILY SEASONAL WORKOUTS
   Fall
   Monday—Weight training program, jog 2-miles on grass

Tuesday—Jog 440, stretch, 6 X 50, 20 minutes triple jump for distance, 40 X 4 phase jumps (H-H-H-J, H-S-S-J, S-H-S-H), 4 X 330

Wednesday—Weight training program, mile on track, increasing speed at each 440, 6 X 100 uphill

Thursday—1-mile jog, stride 50 yard sprints, 4-6 jumps at low height, jump as in competition, jump 35 times in less than 35 minutes at a comfortable (5-8) height. If you clear more than 30, increase by 1" next week, if less than 20, decrease!

Friday—Weight training program, jog 880, stretch, 6 X 220

Saturday—3-6 miles

Sunday—Rest

Winter

Daily warm-up—Jog 880, stretch 10 minutes, 880 sprint-jog

Monday—6 X 1-hurdle, 6 X 4-hurdles, 3 X 200

Tuesday—600-400-200-200-400-600, walk 200 between

Wednesday—20-25 high jumps, hop steps on 1 leg

Thursday—Check approach, 4 X 200

Friday—Competition

Saturday—Competition

Sunday—Rest or jog

Spring

Monday—400-330-220, 4 X 110

Tuesday—Competition or weight training program, 6 X 110

Wednesday—3-step approach at 6-4 to 6-6, 20 X full approach, 10 X 6-0

Thursday—Weight training program—light if competition is Friday, heavy if Saturday

Friday—Competition or hurdle workout

Saturday—Rest or competition

Sunday—25-30 jumps, 6-2 to 6-8 some at 6-10 (not every Sunday)

Summer

Bob competes as often as possible during the summer months.

Peggy Stewart

PEGGY STEWART   Danvers High School

Born 7/31/61   Danvers, Massachusetts

5-11   150   Coach Mike Orechig

COMPETITIVE HISTORY

Massachusetts Track "Athlete of the Year," Peggy has been one of the dominant forces in New England Prep high jumping throughout her high school career. She has Dartmouth Relay, New England High School and AAU and State Meet Championships on her credential list, as well as trips to the AAU and Junior Olympic National Championships.

BEST MARKS
5-8   14.7 (100m h)

AGE GROUP MARKS

Year	Age	HJ
1976	14	5-4
1977	15	5-7
1978	16	5-7
1979	17	5-9

PREPARING FOR COMPETITION

"I don't have any special way of "psyching up," but I am

very competitive. If someone beats me they have to do their best because I always do my best when I am pushed by another competitor."

TRAINING COMMENTS
"I would say that weight work is very important. I also have running workouts; these help me in my high jump and hurdles because it gives me the extra stamina I need. I try to jump about twice a week. I use a nine-step "J" approach."

WEIGHT TRAINING PROGRAM
Peggy has used two different weight training programs.

Junior Year:

Quarter squats	All of the weight on shoulders
Step-ups	3 X 10, 3 times each week
Toe-lifts	Increase weight each week

Senior Year:
Universal Machine and quarter squats, 3 sets of all stations, 1 X 10, 1 X 6, 1 X 3, increase weight on every set. Lift three days a week, increase the weight every day.

DAILY SEASONAL WORKOUTS
Fall
Cross-Country
Winter
Pre-season
Monday—6 X 3 laps (lap = 176 yds), weight training program
Tuesday—4 miles, 8 X 50 strides
Wednesday—Ladder, 2 lap, 3 lap, 4 lap, 3 lap, 2 lap in 35, 38, 40, 38, 35 seconds/lap, 6 X 50 strides
Thursday—2-3 miles, 8 X 50 strides, weight training program
Friday—8 X 660 with 220 recovery, 6 X 50 strides
Saturday—3-5 miles
Sunday—3-5 miles
Everyday, one mile warm-up and one mile

warm-down after track workouts.

Mid-season

Monday—3 sets, 660, 440, 220, with half the distance for recovery

Tuesday—3 miles, jumping for height or technique

Wednesday—8 X 880 at 2:50, 2 lap recovery

Thursday—4 laps with 10 yd recovery
   3 laps with 10 yd recovery
   2 laps with 10 yd recovery

Friday—4 miles, 6 X 50 strides, weight training program

Saturday—3-5 miles

Sunday—3-5 miles

Technique Workout—low heights, great number of jumps, working on steps, arch or snapping and kicking over the bar

Height Workout—Start at 5-feet, take 3 jumps and move up 2 inches, take 3 jumps, move bar up 2 inches until you can no longer clear the bar on all 3 jumps

Spring

Monday—6 X 330, jog-walk 110 recovery

Tuesday—Work on field events, starts, weight training program

Wednesday—3 X 330 in 49 seconds
   3 X 220 in 33 seconds

Thursday—3 miles, technique or height workout, weight training program

Friday—550, 550 race pace, full recovery, 440 race pace, full recovery, 330 race pace

Saturday—3-5 miles

Sunday—3-5 miles

Kenneth Storey

KENNETH STOREY   Plainview High School

Born 11/9/60   Plainview, Texas

6-2 173   Coach Dennis Tomlin

COMPETITIVE HISTORY

Ken went out for track "just to be doing something in the spring season." He has since become the first Texan prep to clear 7-feet.

BEST MARKS

7-0

AGE GROUP MARKS

Year	Age	HJ	100
1975	14	5-1	11.1
1976	15	6-2	10.8
1977	16	6-4	10.2
1978	17	6-6	10.1
1979	18	7-0	10.0

PREPARING FOR COMPETITION

"I just stretch a lot and run to stay loose. The most important thing is how you feel inside, how much you have in your heart."

TRAINING COMMENTS

Ken feels that jumping rope has helped maintain his leg

spring. He has tried to copy Dwight Stones as a basis for his high jumping form.

DAILY SEASONAL WORKOUTS
Fall
  Football
Winter
  Basketball
Spring
  Monday—2 X 220, 2 X 330
  Tuesday—3 X 330, jump 6 times at height
  Wednesday—Jump 6 times at height, 2 X 220, jump rope 1000 reps.
  Thursday—Jump rope, 3 X 330
  Friday—Work on high jump approach
  Saturday—Rest
  Sunday—Jump rope 1000 reps.
Summer
  Everyday—2 X 440, 3 X 100, 3 X 40, 2 X 40 backward, 1 X 440.

Reginald Towns

REGINALD LAMONT TOWNS   Needham B. Broughton H.S.

Born 9/27/61   Raleigh, North Carolina

6-2   180   Coach Ed McLean

COMPETITIVE HISTORY

Now a National Junior Olympic place winner, Reggie got started in track as a seventh grader. He has added State, Regional, Atlanta Youth and East Coast Invitational Championships to an outstanding list of high school accomplishments by working year round on his jumping skills.

BEST MARKS

6-10½   13.9   50.8

AGE GROUP MARKS

Year	Age	HJ	HH
1975	13	5-4	—
1976	14	6-5	—
1977	15	6-10½	15.2
1978	16	6-10	13.9
1979	17	6-9	14.15

PREPARING FOR COMPETITION

"Deep concentration on what I have to do. I compete in

my mind before I actually compete. Sometimes I talk to myself, telling myself what I have to do."

TRAINING COMMENTS
Reggie feels that detailed training, working on specific parts of his jumping technique has been very important to his consistent jumping.

WEIGHT TRAINING PROGRAM
Working out on lifting machines (Universal & Leaper), Reggie lifts 5 days a week in the fall and 2 days each week in winter and spring.

Military Press	Squats
Bench Press	Body Dips
Curls	Leaper Jumps
Leg Curls	Sit-Ups

All lifts done 3 sets of 10, starting with 33% of body weight and increasing 10 to 20 pounds each month.

DAILY SEASONAL WORKOUTS
Fall
Monday-Friday—15 minutes stretching, jump rope, weight training program, approach work in gym, hurdle drills

Winter
Monday—15 minutes stretching, hurdle workout over 5 hurdles, 5 X 60
Tuesday—Weight training program
Wednesday—4 X 440 on time
Thursday—15 minutes stretching, hurdle work, 5 X 60
Friday—Weight training program
Saturday—Rest
Sunday—Rest

Spring
Monday—440 jog, stretch 15 minutes, hurdle drills, 5 X 5 hurdles, 3 X 220 under 24 seconds
Tuesday—440 jog, stretch 15 minutes, jump

workout—20 pop-ups with weighted vest, jump at 5'10"-6'2" with 5 step approach for form, 10 full approach jumps at 6'4"-6'6"

Wednesday—440 jog, stretch 15 minutes, hurdle workout

Thursday—Competition

Friday—440 jog, stretch 15 minutes, hurdle workout, full approach run throughs in high jump

Saturday—Rest

Sunday—Rest

Summer

Monday—440 jog, stretch 15 minutes, hurdle work, speed work

Tuesday—880 jog, stretch 15 minutes, 110's, 220's, 330's, 660's, hurdle work

Wednesday—High jump work on approach and form

Thursday—880 jog, stretch 15 minutes, 110's, 220's, 330's, 660's, hurdle work

Friday—440 jog, stretch 15 minutes, hurdle work, speed work

Saturday—Competition

Sunday—Rest

POLE VAULT

Paul Brattlof

PAUL BRATTLOF

Born 8/16/61

6-0   150

Skyline High School

Dallas, Texas

Coach Joel Ezar

COMPETITIVE HISTORY
The son of a 16-1 vaulter, Paul wanted to try the pole vault to see if he could match his father's performance.

BEST MARKS
16-0

AGE GROUP MARKS

Year	Age	Vault
1976	14	12-0
1977	15	13-9
1978	16	15-2¼
1979	17	16-0

PREPARING FOR COMPETITION
"Just get a good night's sleep before the meet" is Paul's only special preparation.

TRAINING COMMENTS
Paul feels that the running portions of his workouts have been the most important part of his training.

WEIGHT TRAINING PROGRAM

Paul worked out with weights one or two days a week, going for maximum, weight on all lifts.

DAILY SEASONAL WORKOUTS

Fall

Monday—Cross country running
Tuesday—Weight training program, punching bag work, gymnastics
Wednesday—Rest
Thursday—Vault for height
Friday—Sprint workout
Saturday—Vault for height
Sunday—Weight training program, punching bag work, gymnastics

Winter

Monday—Weight training program, sprint workout
Tuesday—Jump rope, punching bag work
Wednesday—Gymnastics
Thursday—Weight training program, sprint workout
Friday—Jump rope, punching bag workout
Saturday—Vault
Sunday—Rest

Paul would try to vault whenever possible during the winter season.

Spring

Monday—Vault, sprint workout, weight training program
Tuesday—Vault, sprint workout, gymnastics
Wednesday—Vault, sprint workout, punching bag work, jump rope
Thursday—Vault
Friday—Rest
Saturday—Competition
Sunday—Rest

Summer

Paul tries to vault whenever possible through the summer.

Jeff Buckingham

JEFF BUCKINGHAM   Gardner High School

Born 6/14/60   Gardner, Kansas

5-7   150   Coach Charles Buckingham

COMPETITIVE HISTORY
Pole vaulting looked like fun when Buckingham went to his first 7th-grade track practice and he's stuck to it since that day. Jeff was named to the adidas & Track and Field News All-America Teams on the basis of a great 1978 season which included a Golden West Invitational win and a 2nd (1st prep) at the Junior A.A.U. Championships.

BEST MARKS
17-½   10.4   5-10

AGE GROUP MARKS

Year	Age	Vault
1973	12	7-6
1974	13	10-½
1975	14	13-4
1976	15	14-9
1977	16	16-0
1978	17	17-½

PREPARING FOR COMPETITION
"I don't have any special way of psyching up for a meet, except I always go to win the meet, regardless of the height of my vault."

TRAINING COMMENTS

Jeff feels his vaulting technique work has been the most important part of his practice, followed by sprint workouts. He vaults for height every day, feeling that this prepares him to face higher heights in big meets.

"I think the reason a lot of high school vaulters don't go as high as they should," says Jeff, "is fear of raising their hand hold. You have to raise your hand hold to go higher."

WEIGHT TRAINING PROGRAM

Jeff had a very low key lifting program, doing bench presses and curls, but on no regular schedule

DAILY SEASONAL WORKOUTS
Fall
Vault seven days a week, weather permitting
Winter
"In winter I don't train; I feel that it's good to have a couple of months lay off from everything after the end of a long season."
Spring
Vault seven days a week, weather permitting, followed by 10 X 100-yard sprints
Summer
"I do a lot of distance work along with vaulting every day. Basically I vault to keep in shape."

Joe Dial

D. JOE DIAL   Marlow High School

Born 1964   Marlow, Oklahoma

5-8½ 130   Coaches Darvis Cole & Dean Dial

COMPETITIVE HISTORY
Starting on a broken pole at age six, Joe has since given up other sports to concentrate on vaulting. State and AAU division champion, he was also the state decathlon champion. In 1980, Joe set a prep record of 17-5¼.

BEST MARKS
17-5¼

AGE GROUP MARKS

Year	Age	Vault
1975	11	8-4
1976	12	9-8
1977	13	13-2
1978	14	14-8
1979	15	16-2¼
1980	16	17-5¼

PREPARING FOR COMPETITION
Joe has no special method of getting ready to compete.

TRAINING COMMENTS
Joe feels that watching films of top vaulters has been an important part of his training. He uses a 107-foot approach, carrying a 15-7 pole with a 14-8 handgrip, varying the pole weight depending on the weather and track.

WEIGHT TRAINING PROGRAM

Joe lifts only lightly, but adds pushups and gymnastics to his strength program.

DAILY SEASONAL WORKOUTS
Fall
Vault every day
Winter
Vault on Monday, Wednesday & Friday
Gymnastics Thursday
Watch films every day
Spring & Summer
Vault every day

Greg Duplantis

GREG DUPLANTIS	Lafayette High School
Born 1/22/62	Lafayette, Louisiana
5-7 140	Coach Charles Lancon

COMPETITIVE HISTORY

Greg followed his brother's footsteps in trying the pole vault and excelled to the point of becoming the National Junior Olympic Champion and Louisiana State record holder. He was invited to participate in the 1978 USOC Pole Vault Training Camp.

BEST MARKS
16-6   10.2

AGE GROUP MARKS

Year	Age	Vault
1975	13	11-0
1976	14	12-6
1977	15	14-6
1978	16	16-0
1979	17	16-6
1980	18	17-0

PREPARING FOR COMPETITION

Greg has no special method of preparing for meets.

TRAINING COMMENTS

"I use the stiffest pole I can handle and attack the box, even to the point of, at times, being out of control. I use a low (14-0 gross) hand hold and rely on a strong push off for high heights."

WEIGHT TRAINING PROGRAM

Greg worked out with weights three days a week, Fall, Winter and Spring.

Squats	2 sets of 6	295#-315#
Bench Press	3 sets of 6, 4 & 2	185#-195#-210#
Dead Lift	3 sets of 6, 4 & 2	275#-295#-305#
Military Press	3 sets of 6, 4 & 2	115#-125#-135#
Cleans	3 sets of 6, 4 & 2	135#-155#-175#

DAILY SEASONAL WORKOUTS

Fall

Monday—Weight training program, stretch, jog 1-hour
Tuesday—Outside sports, stretch, 6 X 100
Wednesday—Weight training program, stretch, jog 1-hour
Thursday—Outside sports, stretch, 6 X 100
Friday—Weight training program, stretch, jog 1-hour
Saturday—Rest
Sunday—Rest

Winter

Monday—Weight training program, stretch, jog mile, 6 X 110, quick steps
Tuesday—Stretch, jog mile, vault 35 jumps
Wednesday—Weight training program, stretch, jog mile, 6 X 220, quick steps
Thursday—Stretch, jog mile, vault 35 jumps
Friday—Weight training program, stretch, jog mile, 6 X 220, quick steps
Saturday—Rest
Sunday—Rest

Spring

Monday—Weight training program, stretch, jog mile
Tuesday—Competition
Wednesday—Weight training program, stretch, jog mile, 6 X 220, quick steps
Thursday—Stretch & jog
Friday—Competition
Saturday—Weight training program, stretch, jog mile, 6 X 220, quick steps
Sunday—Rest

Summer

Greg vaults as often as possible during the summer.

Greg Ernst

GREG ERNST   El Dorado High School

Born 8/14/60   Placentia, California

5-10   163   Coach Don Chadez

COMPETITIVE HISTORY

Greg had little early interest in track, but as a freshman he decided to follow up the football season by trying track as a sprinter. He picked up vaulting, found success, and dropped football to concentrate on track.

As a junior, Greg was 5th in the 1977 California State Meet and was AAU Age Group State Champion. In 1978 he was state runner-up, 3rd at the International Prep Invitational. and 2nd prep at the Junior AAU's. Greg was named to the 1978 *Track and Field News* and Adidas All-American teams.

BEST MARKS
16-6   9.9

AGE GROUP MARKS

Year	Age	Vault	100
1975	14	10-0	12.0
1976	15	13-6	10.7
1977	16	15-7	10.2
1978	17	16-6	9.9

PREPARING FOR COMPETITION

"I do not really have any methods for psyching up; the meet itself does that. I do have one advantage over most high school vaulters. A chiropractor, Dr. Richard Burrhus, a colleague of Dr. Perry's, spends a lot of time with me. Before a big meet he will balance my muscles and basically tune my body up for the meet. I feel this has a very positive effect on my performances."

TRAINING COMMENTS

"There is no one important part of anybody's training. I feel it is the overall program that makes a vaulter. The most important thing is to have a good overall program which consists of endurance work, strength, speed, and technique."

Greg feels strongly about pacing the year's workouts so that peak heights are reached at the end of the spring season. His early work consists of approach and plant drills. During the winter he will vault twice a week, taking 30-40 vaults a day at 14' with a 13' hand hold. He feels this is important to build consistence and confidence. In late spring Greg will vault twice a week at high heights, taking a maximum of 10 vaults each day.

WEIGHT TRAINING PROGRAM

Overhead Press	3-5 sets of 10
Rack Squats	3-5 sets of 5
Toe Raisers	2 sets of maximum amount
Bench Press	3-5 sets of 5
Sit Ups	3 sets of maximum amount
Leg Extension	3 sets of 10
Leg Curls	2 sets of 15

DAILY SEASONAL WORKOUT
Fall
Monday—Weight training program, 3-4 miles
Tuesday—1 mile warmup, 110 strides, high knee lifts
Wednesday—Weight training program, 3-4 miles
Thursday—1 mile warmup, pole runs, plant drills
Friday—Weight training program, 3-4 miles

Saturday—5-6 miles
Sunday—Rest

Winter

Monday—Weight training program, sprint workout, 6 X 330

Tuesday—Warmup, pole run, plant drills, light vaulting

Wednesday—Weight training program, sprint workout, 6 X 330

Thursday—Warmup, vault with short run, low grip, 30 or more vaults

Friday—Weight training program, sprint workout, 6 X 330

Saturday—Run distance

Sunday—Rest

Spring

Monday—Weight training program, pole run, sprint workout, 6 X 220 fast

Tuesday—Vault, leave the bar at a height you have to work on to make, but can make on good vaults

Wednesday—Warmup, stretch, 6 X 110 easy

Thursday—Competition

Friday—Stretch, light 100 yd. strides

Saturday—Competition

Sunday—Rest

Summer

"I work out with the cross-country team, running 5-8 miles, 5 times a week. I will also fit in some pole runs once a week."

Bubba Kavanaugh

BUBBA KAVANAUGH

Oak Park High School

Born 2/21/60

Kansas City, Missouri

5-11   152

Coach Jerry Crews

COMPETITIVE HISTORY

Introduced to pole vaulting in 7th-grade gym class, Bubba stuck with it and has become East Coast and AAU age-group champion as well as Indoor and Outdoor State Champion.

BEST MARKS

16-3

AGE GROUP MARKS

Year	Age	Vault
1974	13	9-6
1975	14	12-6
1976	15	13-0
1977	16	14-6
1978	17	15-3
1979	18	16-4

PREPARING FOR COMPETITION

"I just think to myself what I have to do and how to get it done."

TRAINING COMMENTS

"The most important part of my training was being able

to vault as much as possible. Nothing takes the place of repeated vaulting. Also, I feel it is very important that an athlete has a chance to try the event at an early age. I feel I was fortunate to try the vault in 7th grade. I wish it would have been earlier.

"A big help is being able to have different weight poles so I will have the right ones to jump on." Bubba generally jumps on a 16/175 pole.

WEIGHT TRAINING PROGRAM
Three days per week

Rows, Military Press, Bench Press, Curls, 3 X 10, increase weights 5 to 10 pounds each set.

DAILY SEASONAL WORKOUTS
Fall
Football
Winter
Monday—Sprint workout, weight training program
Tuesday—20-30 run throughs and plants
Wednesday—Sprint workout, weight training program
Thursday—20-30 run throughs and plants at a bar
Friday—Light sprint workout, weight training program
Saturday—Jog
Sunday—Jog
Spring
Monday—Work on approach and plant at a bar, weight training program
Tuesday—Ladder, 110, 220, 330, 440
Wednesday—Jump at a bar with a light pole, weight training program
Thursday—Sprint workout
Friday—Light workout on small poles, weight training program
Saturday—Rest
Sunday—Rest
Summer
Bubba continues his Spring program, but tries to vault more often.

Mark Klee

MARK KLEE   Olathe High School

Born 2/24/62   Olathe, Kansas

5-10   150   Coach Mike Wallace

COMPETITIVE HISTORY
Mark started vaulting in the 8th grade and has been nationally ranked in his age group throughout his career.

BEST MARKS
15-4

AGE GROUP MARKS

Year	Age	Vault
1976	14	10-6
1977	15	13-1¾
1978	16	15-1
1979	17	15-4
1980	18	16-6

PREPARING FOR COMPETITION
"About a week or so before any big meet I really start thinking about my vaulting all the time . . . The day of the meet I don't talk much and like to go off somewhere by myself where I can really think about vaulting. I don't usually vault one or two days before a meet because it makes me more anxious to vault in the meet."

TRAINING COMMENTS
"The most important part of my training is getting all

the practice I can. I practice every chance I can, and have even vaulted in the snow." Mark vaults on Cata-pole, Pacer, and Fiber Sport poles, using a 14-4 handhold and 100-foot approach.

WEIGHT TRAINING PROGRAM

During the winter, Mark lifts four days a week on a machine. Every other day is an "arms" or "legs" day, going all the way around the machine doing 3 sets on every station using just arms or legs.

DAILY SEASONAL WORKOUTS

Fall
    Everyday—Run, stretch, form vaulting
Winter
    Monday-Thursday—Weight training program and run 2-4 miles—vault every day possible, according to the weather.
Spring
    Everyday—Run, stretch, vault
Summer
    Mark vaults every day he can during the summer, sometimes twice a day. He concentrates on form, vaulting for height 2 or 3 days a week.

Bill Lange

BILL LANGE	Bridgewater East High School
Born 1/16/63	Bridgewater, New Jersey
5-10 150	Coaches Ed Ginty & Paul Richards

COMPETITIVE HISTORY
The Age Group World Record holder for 14 and 15 year olds, Bill was introduced to the vault by Paul Richards, an AAU Masters vaulter. A top placer in many Eastern invitationals, Bill has become one of the leading prep vaulters in the country.

BEST MARKS
16-0 6-5

AGE GROUP MARKS

Year	Age	Vault	HJ
1977	14	15-6	
1978	15	16-0	6-5
1979	16	15-0	6-5
1980	17	17-0i	

PREPARING FOR COMPETITION
Bill gets ready by running and high jumping before he has to vault.

TRAINING COMMENTS
Working on pole vault technique has been the most important part of Bill's training.

52

WEIGHT TRAINING PROGRAM
Bill does not lift weights.

DAILY SEASONAL WORKOUTS
Fall and Winter
Monday—Rest
Tuesday—Vault, or work on trampoline
Wednesday—Rest
Thursday—Vault
Friday—Rest
Saturday—Run stadium steps
Sunday—Rest
Spring
Monday—Sprint workout
Tuesday—Vault, sprint workout
Wednesday—Relax, light running workout
Thursday—Vault sprint workout
Friday—Relax, light running workout
Saturday—Relax, light running workout
Sunday—Rest
Summer
Bill vaulted in a few meets, but had trouble practicing due to a lack of facilities. He attended the 1978 USOC Training Camp.

Tim McIntyre

TIM McINTYRE   Los Alamitos High School

Born 10/7/60   Los Alamitos, California

5-9 135   Coach Jim Kanobi

COMPETITIVE HISTORY
Tim started out in track as a distance runner, but switched to the pole vault as a freshman.

BEST MARKS
16-0

AGE GROUP MARKS

Year	Age	Vault
1976	15	12-0
1977	16	14-10
1978	17	15-6
1979	18	16-0

PREPARING FOR COMPETITION
Tim had no special method of getting ready for meets.

TRAINING COMMENTS
McIntyre feels his vaulting technique work has been most important in his training.

WEIGHT TRAINING PROGRAM
"I started lifting weights this summer and I am now

taking a weight lifting class at school, we lift three days a week for about 45 minutes." This is an overall strength program using the basic lifts.

DAILY SEASONAL WORKOUTS
Fall
Monday—Weight training program, swim, run distance, pullups

Tuesday—Gymnastics class

Wednesday—Weight training program, high jump, swim and dive, pullups

Thursday—Rest

Friday—Weight training program, swim or run, pullups

Saturday—Vault, if possible

Sunday—Rest

Winter
Monday—Weight training program, dive, pullups

Tuesday—Gymnastics class

Wednesday—Weight training program, dive, jump rope, pullups

Thursday—Rest

Friday—Weight training program, run distance, pullups

Saturday—Vault, if possible

Sunday—Vault, if possible

Tim is a diver on the swim team during the winter season

Spring
Monday—Weight training program, vault, run high hurdle workout, pullups, dips

Tuesday—Easy vaulting, light lifting, gymnastics class

Wednesday—Rest

Thursday—Competition, weight training program, pullups

Friday—Rest

Saturday—Competition, pullups

Sunday—Rest

Summer
Tim lifts weights for strength during the summer.

Mike Mullins

MIKE MULLINS   James Bowie High School

Born 4/22/60   Arlington, Texas

5-8 130   Coach Ronnie Robertson

COMPETITIVE HISTORY

Going to practice with his father, head coach at Graham H.S., Texas, gave Mike his early interest in track and field. As all coaches know, anyone who hangs around long enough will eventually give pole vaulting a try; Mike used this early start to develop into a consistent, top-performing vaulter.

BEST MARKS
15-3½

AGE GROUP MARKS

Year	Age	Vault
1972	12	8-6
1973	13	9-6
1974	14	10-0
1975	15	11-6
1976	16	13-6
1977	17	15-2
1978	18	15-3½

PREPARING FOR COMPETITION

"There are no really special methods I use. After one meet is over, I usually start thinking about the next one and how I can improve my performance."

TRAINING COMMENTS

"I feel that the weights and speed work are the most important part of training. I also feel that jumping for height in practice improves your form instead of jumping constantly at the lower heights."

WEIGHT TRAINING PROGRAM

Mike worked out on a Universal Gym, doing 70% of maximum on the bench press and military press. He would also do high repetitions of dips, curls, and pull-to-chin exercises.

DAILY SEASONAL WORKOUTS

Fall

Monday & Wednesday—Run 1-mile, weight training program, workout on rope

Tuesday—Run 2-3 miles, tennis or basketball

Thursday—Run 2-3 miles, tennis or basketball

Friday—Weight training program, running with pole

Saturday & Sunday—Rest

Winter

Monday—Weight training program, run 1-mile, 10 X 110

Tuesday—220's, 10 X 110's, run with pole

Wednesday—Weight training program, run 1-mile, 10 X 110

Thursday—220's, 10 X 110's, run with pole

Friday—Weight training program

Saturday—Run distance

Sunday—Rest

Spring

Monday—Jump 20-30 times for height

Tuesday—Jump 15-20 times for height

Wednesday—Jump as on a competition day

Thursday—Jog and loosen up and rest

Friday—Stretch and rest

Saturday—Competition

Sunday—Rest

Summer

Mike competes in summer meets every week, but works out mainly with distance running as summer jobs prevent a regular vault workout program.

Eric Richard

ERIC RICHARD

Born 2/5/63

5-5   150

Bridgewater East High School

Bridgewater, New Jersey

Coaches Ed Ginty & Paul Richard

COMPETITIVE HISTORY

It's easy to get involved in track when your father is a Masters AAU pole vaulter and pentathlon champion. Eric started with the pole vault on a bamboo pole in the backyard. Since that start, he has become one of the top young prep vaulters in the country.

BEST MARKS
15-1

AGE GROUP MARKS

Year	Age	Vault
1973	10	9-6
1974	11	10-6
1975	12	11-6
1976	13	12-0
1977	14	13-6
1978	15	15-1

PREPARING FOR COMPETITION

Eric prepared for meets "just by knowing I have jumped

well in practice before the meet and having had good workouts." Have a good breakfast and a new pair of tube socks."

TRAINING COMMENTS
Eric feels that jumping nine months a year has been the most important part of his training.

WEIGHT TRAINING PROGRAM
Everyday—100 push-ups, 100 sit-ups
Fall—three days a week
Bench press, sit-ups with #10 behind head on slant board, ¾ squats 1 X 10 (#200), dips on bar
Winter—two days a week
Lat-work (#140), military press (#160), curls (#100)
Leg risers on wall ladders 3 X 10

DAILY SEASONAL WORKOUTS
Fall
Football, weight training program three days each week
Winter
Monday—Weight training program
Tuesday—Vault for height, sprint workout
Wednesday—Diving or gymnastics
Thursday—Vault for technique & height, sprint workout
Friday—Weight training program
Saturday—Rest or competition
Sunday—Vault, sprint workout
Spring
Monday—Run long distance
Tuesday—Competition
Wednesday—Sprint workout, 5 X 220 (285) 5 X 440 (60) 7 X 100 (12)
Thursday—Competition
Friday—Run long distance
Saturday—Competition
Sunday—Vault for 2 hours
Summer
Eric vaulted in meets whenever possible, working out with vaulting, sprinting or stair running two nights a week.

LONG JUMP
TRIPLE JUMP

Donnie Butler

DONNIE BUTLER   Fremont High School

Born 6/18/59   Los Angeles, California

5-10   156   Coach Dick Gatlin

COMPETITIVE HISTORY

Coach Gatlin was watching a pickup basketball game when he saw Donnie stuff the ball backwards. He convinced Butler, a junior with 43-inch vertical jump ability, to go out for the track team. By the end of the 1978 season, Donnie had developed into the number one prep long jumper in the country. He adds to his list of credentials a Canada-U.S.A.-Japan Tri-Meet Championship, 2nd place in the 1978 Golden West Invitational and 1978 *Track & Field News* and Adidas All-American honors.

BEST MARKS
25-4   9.4   21.2

AGE GROUP MARKS

Year	Age	LJ	100	220
1977	17	24-11¾	9.9	21.9
1978	18	25-4	9.4	21.2

PREPARING FOR COMPETITION

"Normally I'm an extrovert. I enjoy life, I'm carefree and loose. Just before competition I'm calm, not tense, not scared, but ready to compete."

62

TRAINING COMMENTS

Donnie claims that his practice was sometimes "a little loose"—he was "distracted by Fremont's Girls Track Team." He credits his top performances to competing with a great 1977 team and to experience in international competition. The most important part of his 1978 training was "a steady diet of 400-, 300-, and 200-yard runs and improving my approach."

WEIGHT TRAINING PROGRAM

As a junior, Donnie says he "snuck out of weights," but did some light lifting during the 1978 season.

DAILY SEASONAL WORKOUTS

Fall

Football

Winter

Monday—Jog 2 miles, stretch, warm down

Tuesday—Easy 1320 under 5 minutes

Wednesday—Jog 2 miles, stretch, warm down

Thursday—Stride 8 X 220

Friday—110's on grass

Saturday—Rest

Sunday—Rest.

Spring

Monday—Block work, relay pass work, 4 X 150

Tuesday—Runway 6 times for steps, 2 X 660

Wednesday—Team challenges, 400 yards in 43.8, 6 X 100 easy, 300 yards in 31.9, walk lap, 200 yards in 20.9

Thursday—Relay practice

Friday—Competition

Saturday—Invitational competition

Sunday—Rest

Summer

"Compete as often as possible during the week, rest on Friday, competition on Saturday, rest on Sunday."

Ken Fowler

KENNETH FOWLER

Fontana High School

Born 8/24/60

Fontana, California

5-9   153

Coach Pickett

COMPETITIVE HISTORY
Ken's early interest in track and field came from elementary school meets in the Fontana School District. Nationally ranked as a sprinter, Ken is looking to move into the long jump ranking.

BEST MARKS
23-11   9.5

PREPARING FOR COMPETITION
"I just like to know I have my muscles trained to do the job."

TRAINING COMMENTS
"Stretching is the most important part of my workout for long jumping. I do lots of situps and stretching so that I can be warmed up enough to have my step exactly on the mark."

WEIGHT TRAINING PROGRAM
Squats	3 X 15	160#
Leg Curls	3 X 15	50#
Arm Curls	3 X 15	40#

DAILY SEASONAL WORKOUTS
Fall and Winter
Monday—Overdistance
Tuesday—Weight training program, sit-ups
Wednesday—Sprint work
Thursday—Overdistance
Friday—Weight training program, sit-ups
Saturday—Sprint work
Sunday—Rest
Spring
Monday—3 X 330
Tuesday—3 X 350, 3 X 220, 3 X 165
Wednesday—Light running work
Thursday—3 X 330
Friday—3 X 350, 3 X 220, 3 X 165
Saturday—Light running work
Summer
Ken concentrates on weight training through the summer.

David Hintz

DAVID HINTZ   Custer High School

Born 9/5/63   Milwaukee, Wisconsin

6-0   158   Coach Marsh Potter

COMPETITIVE HISTORY

The National sophomore indoor record holder in the long jump, David began by watching his uncle at meets, then trying some jumping after the meets were over.

BEST MARKS
23-6

AGE GROUP MARKS

Year	Age	LJ	Decathlon
1977	13	20-7¾	
1978	14	22-3	
1979	15	23-6	
1980	16	––	5625

PREPARING FOR COMPETITION

"The night before a meet I watch films of the good guys—Beamon and the others. The day of the meet, just before I am ready to jump, I go through my whole jump in my mind, thinking of good speed, height at the take-off board, and a good landing."

TRAINING COMMENTS

David feels that working on leg quickness through weight training, running stairs, hurdles and sprints has been a big part of his success. He uses a 114-8 approach, with a checkmark four steps down the runway.

WEIGHT TRAINING PROGRAM

Squats	2 X 10	120#
Leg curls	3 X 10	60#
Front extension		
leg lifts	3 X 20	60#

DAILY SEASONAL WORKOUTS

Fall

Football

Winter

Monday—1 mile warmup, stretch, weight training
Tuesday—1 mile warmup, stretch, run hurdles
Wednesday—Run distance, stretch, weight training
Thursday—1 mile warmup, stretch, run stairs for 30 minutes
Friday—1 mile warmup, stretch
Saturday—Competition
Sunday—Rest

Spring

Monday—1 mile run, stretch, 7-10 LJ run-throughs, run hurdles, weight training program
Tuesday—1 mile run, stretch, 7-10 LJ run-throughs, 3-5 jumps, run hurdles
Wednesday—1 mile run, stretch, 220's, run stairs
Thursday—1 mile run, stretch, run hurdles, 3-7 jumps
Friday—Run distance, stretch
Saturday—Competition
Sunday—Rest

Summer

Monday—Warmup, stretch, 7-10 LJ run-throughs, run hurdles
Tuesday—Warmup, stretch, sprint workout
Wednesday—Warmup, stretch, LJ box jumping drills, run hurdles
Thursday—Warmup, stretch, run hurdles
Friday—Warmup, stretch
Saturday—Competition
Sunday—Rest

Ricky Holliday

RICKY HOLLIDAY   John Muir High School

Born 8/6/62   Pasadena, California

6-3   175   Coach Walter Opp

COMPETITIVE HISTORY

Ricky became involved in track as a seventh grader and has stayed with it exclusively through high school. A league champion and all star, he has been a medal winner in the California State Meet.

BEST MARKS

48-11¾   23-4½   22.3

AGE GROUP MARKS

Year	Age	TJ	LJ	100	220
1976	13	——	18-11½	10.5	——
1977	14	——	20-10	10.1	23.0
1978	15	43-2	23-4½	9.9	22.6
1979	16	48-11¾	23-2½	——	22.3
1980	17	51-3	——	——	——

PREPARING FOR COMPETITION

'I just try not to think about the meet. All week before a big meet I try to have as much fun as possible . . . I stay this way during the meet. On the runway I change. I'm still feeling good, but I concentrate on the board and on speed and height."

TRAINING COMMENTS
Ricky feels he has been helped by reading about other jumpers and by watching the technique and style of top performers.

WEIGHT TRAINING
Holliday has no organized weight training program, but does some light lifting in the off season.

DAILY SEASONAL WORKOUTS
Fall
Cross-Country
Winter
Nothing
Spring
Everyday—Warm up with 1 mile run, stretch, 880 run, stretch
Monday—Warm up, 10 approach runs, long jump once or twice for distance
Tuesday—Warm up, triple jump, over 46-0—3 times, try for 50-0 once
Wednesday—Warm up, run easy 440, stretch
Thursday—Competition
Friday—Work on problems from meet, runway approach, jump height form work
Saturday—Rest
Sunday—Jog
Summer
Ricky works out during the summer to stay in shape and competes in area AAU meets.

Willie Houston

WILLIE RAY HOUSTON   Mt. Pleasant High School

Born 1/5/60   Mt. Pleasant, Texas

6-3   185   Coach Mike Field

COMPETITIVE HISTORY
A track man since junior high and an all district basketball player, Willie was district champ in the 220 and long jump. He won the Texas State Long Jump Championship in 1978.

BEST MARKS
24-10   21.4   9.7

AGE GROUP MARKS

Year	Age	LJ	220	100
1974	14	16-0	——	12.5
1975	15	21-8	——	10.5
1976	16	22-4½	22.7	10.1
1977	17	23-2	21.9	9.9
1978	18	24-10	21.4	9.7
1979	19	23-10	——	——

PREPARING FOR COMPETITION
"Before my event, I try to get the feel of the track. After I loosen up, I lie down and think about the event and who I'm going to compete against."

TRAINING COMMENTS
Willie feels the biggest part of his success has come from the extra practice time he has put into his events.

WEIGHT TRAINING PROGRAM
"I lift weights when possible. I lift light weights, just enough to maintain my strength."

DAILY SEASONAL WORKOUTS
Fall
Monday—Warm up, run 440, jog 880, run 220, 60 bench jumps, jump rope, run bleachers

Tuesday—Warm up, run 880, walk 220, run 220, walk 440, run 440, jump rope, 75 bench jumps, run 100 bleachers

Wednesday—Warm up, jog 1 mile, walk 440, run 440, walk 440, jog 1 mile, 75 bench jumps, run 50 bleachers

Thursday—Warm up, run 880-440-220, jump rope, 50 bench jumps

Friday—Rest

Saturday—Rest

Sunday—Rest

Winter
Basketball

Spring
Monday—Loosen up and stretch, 4 X 330, 6 X 100, 10 pop-ups, run through and check steps

Tuesday—8 X 220, 10 pop-ups, check steps, 50 bench jumps

Wednesday—Practice starts, 10 X 150, 10 pop-ups, 50 bench jumps

Thursday—10 X 100 on grass, check steps

Friday—Competition

Saturday—Run distance

Sunday—Run distance

Summer
Willie worked out in the summer running pick up races in the park, running 10 miles a day distance and doing bench jumps.

Andre Kirnes

ANDRE KIRNES

Born 2/1/61

5-10   145

Northeast High School

St. Petersburg, Florida

Coach Dave Derrick

COMPETITIVE HISTORY

An eighth grade P.E. teacher saw Andre's talent and recommended he try out for the track team. He enjoyed it, and gave up other sports to concentrate on jumping and hurdling skills.

BEST MARKS
25-2½   14.0

AGE GROUP MARKS

Year	Age	LJ
1975	14	17-9
1976	15	21-7
1977	16	injured
1978	.17	24-1¼
1979	18	25-2½

PREPARING FOR COMPETITION

"I don't exactly psych up. I just try to put to use everything I learned in practice, with every bit of effort."

TRAINING COMMENTS

Andre feels that his drills, especially pop-ups while

working leg motions and hurdling, have been the most help. He also worked hard with step-ups and stadium hops.

WEIGHT TRAINING PROGRAM

Andre's weight program concentrated on leg strength. Step-ups (#130, increase #5 every 2 weeks), leg press, and leg curls, stretching and running distance with each workout.

DAILY SEASONAL WORKOUTS

Fall

Monday—Weight training program, long jump drills, run-throughs, hurdle drills, jog 2 miles

Tuesday—Long jump drills, hurdle drills

Wednesday—Weight training program, long jump drills, jog 2 miles

Thursday—Long jump drills, run distance

Friday—Long jump drills, run distance

Saturday & Sunday—Run 2 miles

Winter

Monday—Weight training program, run distance

Tuesday—Long jump drills, hurdle drills, stadium hops

Wednesday—Weight training program, run distance

Thursday—Long jump drills, hurdle drills, stadium hops

Friday—Weight training program, run distance

Saturday & Sunday—Run 3-4 miles

Spring

Monday—Long jump drills, work hurdles, 550, 440, 330 sets

Tuesday—Long jump drills, work hurdles, stadium hops, 550, 440, 330 sets

Wednesday—Long jump drills, work hurdles, 550, 440, 330 sets

Thursday—Long jump drills, work hurdles, stadium hops, 550, 440, 330 sets

Friday—Long jump drills, work hurdles, 550, 440, 330 sets

Saturday—Run 2 miles

Sunday—Run 2 miles

Summer

Kirnes did a great deal of distance running during the summer, concentrating on leg strength, working very little on long jumping.

Carl Lewis

CARL LEWIS   Willingboro High School

Born 7/1/61   Willingboro, New Jersey

6-1   165   Coach Minore

COMPETITIVE HISTORY

Starting as a seven-year-old in his parents' track club, Carl developed into one of the top prep long jumpers and sprinters in the nation, finishing second in the 1979 AAU Championships.

BEST MARKS

26-6½   44-11½   9.3   21.5

AGE GROUP MARKS

Year	Age	LJ	TJ	100	220
1974	13	17-6	35-9	11.5	25.2
1975	14	18-7	38-10	11.2	24.0
1976	15	20-0	40-1	11.0	23.5
1977	16	22-6	44-1	10.4	22.8
1978	17	25-9	44-11½	9.3	21.5
1979	18	26-6½	——	9.5	20.9

PREPARING FOR COMPETITION

"I don't do anything special. I think the key to my performances is relaxation. I always think that I can compete with anyone at any time no matter how good the

competition. I do not talk much with my competitors during competition, but often do afterwards."

TRAINING COMMENTS

Carl enjoys training with a teammate. "My track team members make it easy for me, because they really look up to me and ask a lot of questions. It just makes me proud to answer and run with them."

WEIGHT TRAINING PROGRAM

Carl used a light, overall program, lifting three days a

week through October only.

DAILY SEASONAL WORKOUTS
September—No Training

October—Monday—Weight training program
Tuesday—2-5 miles
Wednesday—Weight training program
Thursday—2-5 miles
Friday—Weight training program
Saturday—Rest
Sunday—Rest

Winter
Early Season
Monday—Long intervals (440-880)
Tuesday—2-5 miles
Wednesday—Long intervals (440-880)
Thursday—2-5 miles
Friday—Long intervals (440-880)
Saturday—Form jumping
Sunday—Rest

Late Season
Monday—Short intervals (60, 110, 220, 440)
Tuesday—Starts, short runs
Wednesday—Short intervals (60, 110, 220, 440)
Thursday—Starts, short runs
Friday—Short intervals (60, 110, 220, 440)
Saturday—Fartlek
Sunday—Rest

Spring
Monday—Sprint work
Tuesday—Form jumping, block starts
Wednesday—Sprint ladder (110-220-440-220-110)
Thursday—Form jumping, block starts
Friday—Stretching & loosening up
Saturday—Competition
Sunday—Rest

Summer
Carl worked out on Tuesdays and Thursdays, doing a sprint workout and form jumping.

Ernest Marvin

ERNEST MARVIN

Spring Valley High School

Born 6/7/59

Columbia, South Carolina

5-7½ 149

Coach Mike Bozeman

COMPETITIVE HISTORY

Ernest tried out for the track team when he had nothing else to do as a ninth grader. He made the team and everything went uphill from there. In 1978, Marvin was the Atlanta Classic champion, was 2nd in the Golden West Invitational, 2nd in the International Prep Invitational and was named to the Adidas and *Track & Field News* All American teams.

BEST MARKS

51-7 23-8½ 10.9(m) 49.5

AGE GROUP MARKS

Year	Age	LJ	TJ
1975	15	20-6	——
1976	16	23-8½	46-7
1977	17	23-5¼	49-1¼
1978	18	23-6½	51-7

PREPARING FOR COMPETITION

"The only methods of psyching up or getting ready for competition is a great deal of concentration before each jump."

TRAINING COMMENTS

Ernest felt that the most important part of his training was bounding with a weight vest.

WEIGHT TRAINING PROGRAM

Marvin used very little weight lifting in his training. He did use resistance exercises as running steps, bounding with a weight vest, and depth jumping.

DAILY SEASONAL WORKOUTS

Fall

No fall training

Winter

Monday—Warmup, 2 X 550, 3 X 220, warm down

Tuesday—Warmup relay practice, bounding drills with weight vest, 20 X 50 yds (R-R-L-L), 10 X 100, warm down

Wednesday—Warmup, 10 X LJ pop-ups with 6 stride approach, 10 X TJ with 5 stride approach, 3 X 330, warm down (emphasis height on all pop-up drills)

Thursday—Warmup, relay practice, bounding drills (same as Tuesday)

Friday—Warmup, 10 X LJ pop-ups with 6 stride approach, 6 X 220, warmdown

Saturday & Sunday—Rest

Spring

Monday—Warmup, relay practice, 10 X approach run working on speed and relaxation

Tuesday—Competition

Wednesday—Warmup, relay practice, 30 minutes of box drills, 330-220-110

Thursday—Warmup, 10 X LJ pop-ups with 50 foot approach, 10 X 50 yards of hops on each leg, 10 X approach run

Friday—Warmup, relay practice, check steps, jog 880

Saturday—Major competition

Sunday—Rest

Summer

Ernest works out with easy running and light bounding during the summer, competing in the Junior Olympics program or other invitational meets.

Keith Richardson

KEITH A. RICHARDSON   Bryan Station High School

Born 4/28/61   Lexington, Kentucky

5-11   165   Coach Paul Woodall

COMPETITIVE HISTORY

A junior high school sprinter, Keith got started in track in age group "Little Olympics" meets. Third in the Kentucky State long jump, as well as triple jump champion, he has progressed steadily, becoming one of the top horizontal jumpers in the nation.

BEST MARKS

49-3   22-10

AGE GROUP MARKS

Year	Age	TJ	LJ
1975	14	36-10	17-1½
1976	15	37-11	17-9
1977	16	45-3	22-3
1978	17	49-3	22-10
1979	18	48-10	——

PREPARING FOR COMPETITION

"I go somewhere off by myself before and during the day of the meet and think about what I'm going to do. Everything else leaves my mind. I'll picture myself going

through the jump and getting a good jump. Triple and long jumping is something I really enjoy so I get excited about it, which helps me to perform."

TRAINING COMMENTS

Keith credits Coach Woodall's teaching and his own strong mental attitude for his success. His determination and will-to-win have pushed him to train hard to reach his goals.

WEIGHT TRAINING PROGRAM

Keith worked out during winter and spring with a leg strength, arm power program.

DAILY SEASONAL WORKOUTS

Fall

Football

Winter

Warm weather; every day—outdoors

Warmup with 440 stretch, run 1 mile, run stadium steps pumping arms, 4 X 50 yard sprints with form running or form jumping between each sprint, 440 warm down

Cold weather; every day—indoors

Weight lifting, form jumping, sprints

Play basketball and ride exercise bike on weekends

Spring

Every day

Weight training program, run 440 warmup, stretch, run stadium steps, run 1 mile, run sprints, work on approach and form jumping

Keith played basketball to work on his jumping and ran distance every night.

Summer

Richardson worked out for football during the summer.

Mike Scudieri

MIKE SCUDIERI   Annandale High School

Born 9/27/60   Annandale, Virginia

6-0   155   Coach Marshall Windsor

COMPETITIVE HISTORY
Mike went out for track at his father's urging after having participated in other sports. In four years of track and field competition he developed into one of the top horizontal jumpers in Fairfax County.

BEST MARKS
48-¾   22-4   22.1

AGE GROUP MARKS

Year	Age	TJ	LJ	220
1976	15	36-0	16-3	——
1977	16	42-7	19-1	25.4
1978	17	46-5	21-2½	22.9
1979	18	48-¾	22-4	22.1

PREPARING FOR COMPETITION
"Tough competition makes it easier to 'psych-up'."

TRAINING COMMENTS
Mike feels that pre-season strength work is an important part of triple jump training.

WEIGHT TRAINING PROGRAM

half squats	3 X 10
bench press	3 X 10
curls	3 X 10
military press	3 X 10

DAILY SEASONAL WORKOUTS

Fall

Monday—3 mile run (AM)
2 X 330, 6 X 150, weight training program (PM)
Tuesday—3 mile run (AM)
10 approach runs (PM)
Wednesday—3 mile run (AM)
10 X 150, hops on bleachers, weight training program (PM)
Thursday—3 mile run (AM)
6 X 100 hops on strong leg, 4 X 100 hops on weak leg, 4 x 100 accelerations (PM)
Friday—3 mile run (AM)
6 X 220 accelerations (PM)
Saturday—1 mile run, run bleachers
Sunday—3 mile run

Winter

Monday—4 X 100 yd hops on strong leg, 2 X 100 yd hops on weak leg, 4 X 330 accelerations, weight training program
Tuesday—10 approach runs, pop-ups (15 LJ, 10 TJ), 4 X 165, 4 x 100 accelerations
Wednesday—Bleacher runs, pop-ups (15 LJ, 10 TJ), 12 X 165 accelerations, weight training program
Thursday—10 approach runs, pop-ups (15 LJ, 10 TJ), 3 X 600
Friday—4 X 100 yd hops on strong leg, 2 X 100 yd hops on weak leg, 6 X 220
Saturday—10 approach runs, pop-ups (15 LJ, 10 TJ), 4 X 110 accelerations, weight training program
Sunday—3 mile run

Spring

Monday—4 X 100 yd hops on strong leg, 2 X 100 yd hops on weak leg, 6 X 330 accelerations, weight training program

Tuesday—10 approach runs, pop-ups (15 LJ, 10 TJ), 12 X 165

Wednesday—Bleacher runs, pop-ups (15 LJ, 10 TJ), 1 X (600, 500, 400, 300)

Thursday—10 approach runs, pop-ups (15 LJ, 10 TJ), 4 X 60, 4 X 100, weight training program

Friday—4 X 100 yd hops on strong leg, 2 X 100 yd hops on weak leg, 4 X 660

Saturday—10 approach runs, pop-ups (15 LJ, 10 TJ), 4 X 100

Sunday—3 mile run

Mike eases up before big meet competition, stopping weight training and hop exercises two weeks before district meets.

Summer

Run 3 miles each day, weight training and bleacher runs on alternate days.

Darryl Smith

DARRYL SMITH   Denbigh High School

Born 7/8/60   Newport News, Virginia

6-1   180   Coach Jimmy Hill

COMPETITIVE HISTORY
Darryl turned to track to follow the footsteps of his brother. The Virginia indoor long jump record holder, he triple jumped to 3rd place in the 1978 State meet.

BEST MARKS
23-10¾ 48-¾ 10.0

PREPARING FOR COMPETITION
"I just try to put everything out of my mind and concentrate on what I am doing."

TRAINING COMMENTS
Darryl thinks being in top shape is the key to good performances. He uses the indoor season to build up leg strength and to get into shape, and the spring season to perfect his technique and hit peak form.

WEIGHT TRAINING PROGRAM
Darryl lifted weights during winter and spring on an overall strength program. He also did jumping exercises using a 30 pound weight bag.

DAILY SEASONAL WORKOUTS

Fall
Football

Winter
Monday—Weight training program, jumping exercises, 330's

Tuesday—Running workout

Wednesday—Weight training program, jumping exercises, 600's

Thursday—Light running

Friday—Weight training program, form work on jumping

Saturday—Distance

Sunday—Rest

Spring
Monday—Weight training program, form jumping, 440's

Tuesday—330's

Wednesday—Weight training program, form jumping, 220's

Thursday—Stride 440's at ½ speed

Friday—Form jumping, technique work

Saturday—Distance

Sunday—Rest

Ward Wilson

WARD WILSON   Winston Churchill High School

Born 10/30/59   Potomac, Maryland

5-9   150   Coach Andrew White

COMPETITIVE HISTORY

Elementary school games and jumping over creeks gave Ward an early enjoyment of running and jumping. Encouraged by his parents and teachers, he began long jumping as an eighth grader. The Maryland State record holder in the 60 yard dash, Ward was the Navel Academy Invitational Triple Jump Champion and 3rd in the Maryland State Long Jump.

BEST MARKS

47-4   23-0   9.78   21.9   6.2 (60)

AGE GROUP MARKS

Year	Age	TJ	LJ
1974	14	——	16-10
1976	16	42-11	22-4
1977	17	46-5	22-6
1978	18	46-7 (i)	23-0
		47-4 (o)	

PREPARING FOR COMPETITION

"I get myself ready for competition by being myself in a dark room, listening to music turned up as high as possible.

The feeling that I get stays with me. If I lose it, I have to concentrate on one song that I like and then I will be ready."

TRAINING COMMENTS

Ward feels that his weight training, and keeping in good overall condition, have been the most important parts of his training program.

WEIGHT TRAINING PROGRAM

Ward worked out on a Universal machine, concentrating on overall strength and flexibility.

DAILY SEASONAL WORKOUTS
Fall
Football
Winter and Spring
Monday—15 hops on each leg, 3 flights stairs, bunny hops, 10 X 110 strides, weight training program, 10 hills, jog 880
Tuesday—Bunny hops, 100 yard strides, run distance, practice jumping, run through steps
Wednesday—Weight training program, 10 hills, 10 X hopping on stairs, 2 X 300, 2 X 220, 1 X 100, jog 880
Thursday—10 downhill runs, TJ & LJ with 3-5-7 step approach, 2 full jumps TJ & LJ, stride 100's, jog 880
Friday—Weight training program
Saturday—Form jumping, bunny hops, 100 yard bounds, stride 180's
Sunday—Run distance
Summer
Relax

SHOT PUT
DISCUS THROW

Michael Carter

MICHAEL CARTER   Thomas Jefferson High School

Born 10/29/60   Dallas, Texas

6-2   250   Coach James Neely

COMPETITIVE HISTORY
The premier weightman of the decade, Mike began in track as a sprinter and finished his prep career by setting a new national record in the 12 pound shot and challenging the discus record. He is also the second all-time prep with the 16-pound shot. Winning every championship in sight, the incomparable Carter was a two-time All-America Team member.

BEST MARKS
81-3½ (12#)   67-9 (16#)   204-8

AGE GROUP MARKS

Year	Age	Shot	Discus
1975	14	45 (8#)	
1976	15	70-5	
1977	16	65-11 (12#)	181-9
1978	17	71-1½	193-10
1979	18	81-3½	204-8

PREPARING FOR COMPETITION

"I just put my mind to it. I just try to do my best. I have a certain mark I'd like to achieve in every meet; I write it down—but I don't show it to anyone."

TRAINING COMMENTS

Mike feels that his strength program has been the most important part of his training.

WEIGHT TRAINING PROGRAM

Mike started with a basic, overall strength and conditioning program, but now works out primarily doing cleans, jerks and full squats.

DAILY SEASONAL WORKOUTS

Fall

Football

Winter

Off-season football work, throwing the shot and discus whenever the weather is warm enough to workout outdoors

Spring

Monday—Throw shot and discus, weight training program

Tuesday—Throw shot and discus, weight training program

Wednesday—Throw shot and discus, weight training program

Thursday—Throw shot and discus

Friday—Run, light throwing for form

Saturday—Competition

Sunday—Rest

Summer

Prepare for football

Danny Flatt

DANNY FLATT   Wooddale High School

Born 3/29/60·   Memphis, Tennessee

6-2   230   Coach W.S. Donald

COMPETITIVE HISTORY

As an eighth grader, Dan was introduced to the shot put by his older brother. Since then he has become league, District, city, Regional, and State champion. He ranked among the leading indoor prep shot putters during the 1978 season.

BEST MARKS
61-10   152-3½

AGE GROUP MARKS

Year	Age	Shot
1974	14	45-6½ (#8)
1975	15	59-10½ (#8)
		52-2¼ (#12)
1976	16	53-10½
1977	17	57-6¼
1978	18	61-10

PREPARING FOR COMPETITION

"I use visualization of the throw right before I throw. I eat honey before I throw. I usually wear the same clothes on every meet day; I've worn the same socks and jock for every meet for the past three years."

TRAINING COMMENTS

Danny feels that his weight training program has been the greatest aid to his shot putting success.

WEIGHT TRAINING PROGRAM

Dan uses the bench press, squat and dead lift, 4-5 repetitions at maximum weight.

DAILY SEASONAL WORKOUTS

Fall

Monday—Weight training program, run stairs
Tuesd iy—Jog 880-mile
Wednesday—Weight training program, run sprints
Thursday—Jog, light throwing
Friday—Weight training program, run stairs
Saturday—Basketball
Sunday—Rest

Dan starts off with only half circles and then progresses to full circles and harder throwing as he progresses through the fall season.

Winter

Monday—Weight training program, run sprints
Tuesday—Throw, jog 880-mile
Wednesday—Weight training program, run sprints
Thursday—Throw, jog 880-mile
Friday—Weight training program, run sprints
Saturday—Basketball

Spring

Monday—Weight training program, run sprints
Tuesday—Throw, jog 880-mile
Wednesday—Weight training program, run sprints
Thursday—Throw, run sprints
Friday—Rest
Saturday—Competition
Sunday—Rest

Summer

Dan's summer training was similar to his spring schedule.

Melanie Heitman

MELANIE HEITMAN Williamsburg Community High School

Born 5/13/61   Williamsburg, Iowa

5-11   175   Coach John Cochrane

COMPETITIVE HISTORY
Introduced to the weight events as a freshman, Melanie has been an All-State team member ever since. State record holder and three time discus champion, she is also shot put champion and a Junior Olympic medal winner in the discus and javelin.

BEST MARKS
147-5 (j)   150-1 (d)   41-4 (4k)

AGE GROUP MARKS

Year	Age	Discus	Shot (4k)	Javelin
1976	15	122-10	34-6	——
1977	16	136-5	37-3	——
1978	17	147-5	41-4	149-0
1979	18	150-1	——	

PREPARING FOR COMPETITION
"Thinking through the entire, correct technique and staying as relaxed as possible," is Heitman's preparation regimen.

TRAINING COMMENTS
Melanie feels that her technique work and weight training program especially her greatly increased lifting over the past

two years—have been the most important part of her training.

WEIGHT TRAINING PROGRAM
Melanie uses a complex, 22-week training program using free weights.

PREPARATION PHASE
6 WEEKS (MARCH/APRIL)
2 DAYS/WEEK ON EACH BODY AREA (UPPER, LOWER, JAVELIN)

Sunday—Rest
Monday—Upper
Tuesday—Lower
Wednesday—Javelin lifts
Thursday—Upper
Friday—Lower
Saturday—Javelin lifts

UPPER BODY LIFTS
Bench Press
Incline Bench Press
Jerk
LOWER BODY LIFTS
Cleans
High Pulls
Squats
JAVELIN LIFTS
Lunges 5 X 8
Bent Arm Pullovers 3 X 8
Curls 3 X 8

% SCHEDULE
Upper and lower body lifts are determined by a % of maximum system. Maximums are retested after each lifting phase.

WEEK	SESSION 1	SESSION 2
1	60% 5 X 5	60% 5 X 5
2	65% 5 X 5	60% 5 X 5
3	70% 5 X 5	65% 5 X 5
4	75% 5 X 5	70% 5 X 5
5	80% 5 X 5	75% 5 X 5
6	85% 5 X 5	80% 5 X 5

Lift thru all meets during this phase

COMPETITION PHASE I
6 WEEKS (APRIL-MAY)
3 DAYS/WEEK ON EACH BODY AREA

Sunday—Rest
Monday—Upper

Upper & Lower Body Lifts
Same as preparation phase

Tuesday—Lower & javelin   Javelin lifts
Wednesday—Upper   Curls 3 X 5
Thursday—Lower & javelin   Bent Arm Pullovers 3 X 5
Friday—Upper   (progressive lifting—increase
Saturday—Lower or   weight during this phase)
   competition

% SCHEDULE

WEEK	SESSION 1	SESSION 2	SESSION 3
1	75% 4 X 3	85% 4 X 3	60% 4 X 3
2	80% 4 X 3	85% 5 X 3	60% 4 X 3
3	80% 4 X 3	85% 6 X 3	60% 4 X 3
4	75% 4 X 3	90% 3 X 3	60% 4 X 3
5	75% 4 X 3	90% 4 X 3	60% 4 X 3
6	80% 4 X 3	90% 5 X 3	60% 4 X 3

Minor meets will be lifted thru. If there is one major meet,
stop lifting after Wednesday for a Saturday meet.

COMPETITION PHASE II
6 WEEKS (JUNE-JULY)
3 DAYS/WEEK ON EACH BODY AREA

Sunday—Rest   Upper & Lower body lifts same
Monday—Upper   as Preparation Phase
Tuesday—Lower & javelin   Javelin Lifts
Wednesday—Upper   Curls (3 X 5)
Thursday—Lower & javelin   Bent Arm Pullovers (3 X 5)
Friday—Upper   During the last 2 weeks of this
Saturday—Lower or   phase reduce weight and lift for
   competition   speed

% SCHEDULE

WEEK	SESSION 1	SESSION 2	SESSION 3
1	75% 4 X 2	90% 4 X 2	60% 4 X 3
2	80% 4 X 2	90% 5 X 2	60% 4 X 3
3	80% 4 X 2	90% 6 X 2	60% 4 X 3
4	75% 4 X 2	95% 3 X 2	60% 4 X 3
5	75% 4 X 2	95% 4 X 2	60% 4 X 3
6	80% 4 X 2	95% 5 X 2	60% 4 X 3

Lift thru all but one important meet during this phase.

PEAK PHASE
4 WEEKS (JULY-AUGUST)
2 DAYS/WEEK ON EACH BODY AREA

Sunday—Rest
Monday—Upper
Tuesday—Lower
Wednesday—Rest
Thursday—Upper
Friday—Lower
Saturday—Rest or Competition

Upper Body Lifts
Bench Press
Jerks
Lower Body Lifts
Squats
Cleans

% SCHEDULE

WEEK	SESSION 1	SESSION 2
1	90% 3 X 3	60% 4 X 3
2	new max 3 X 1	60% 4 X 3
3	60% 4 X 3	rest
4	rest and big meet	

DAILY SEASONAL WORKOUTS
Fall
None
Winter
Basketball
Spring
Monday—Weight training program, throw shot, discus drills (no discus)

Tuesday—Weight training program, throw discus, shot drills (no shot)

Wednesday—Weight training program, javelin work

Thursday—Weight training program, throw shot, discus drills

Friday—Weight training program, throw discus, shot drills

Saturday—Weight training program, javelin work
Summer
Spring and summer patterns are much the same, with the number of throws decreasing and sprint lengths shorter as compared to early season.

Jackie Henry

JACKIE HENRY   Lynnwood Senior High School

Born 12/18/61   Lynnwood, Washington

5-9½   170   Coaches Duane Lewis & Ernie Gosshorn

COMPETITIVE HISTORY

Jackie was first introduced to track as an eleven-year-old in an A.A.U. club program. An outstanding all-round athlete, she has become one of the nation's top prep weight performers.

BEST MARKS

50-10½ (8#)   46-6¾ (4k)   154-4 (d)

AGE GROUP MARKS

Year	Age	Shot	Discus
1973	11	30-1	——
1974	12	36-7	——
1975	13	41-11	——
1976	14	45-1	——
1977	15	47-11¾	131-4
1978	16	50-4	140-4
1979	17	50-10½	154-4

PREPARING FOR COMPETITION

"To get ready for competition I take time to concentrate on my form the night before. I try to get a positive mental picture in my mind. I also take care of details the night before so I don't have to worry about them the day

I compete (i.e., fixing lunch, getting my uniform ready, etc.).
I also get plenty of sleep."

TRAINING COMMENTS

"I feel that flexibility, strength, and speed are the three most important factors to develop while training. Technique is pertinent, as these factors rely on technique to utilize them."

WEIGHT TRAINING PROGRAM

Jackie works with free weights, three days each week.

Warm-Up
2 X 10 side bends with weights (30#)
3 X 10 transversals (25#)
1 X 10 sit-ups
1 X 10 rotations (50#)
Major Lifts
3 X 5 Cleans (95#)
3 X 5 Snatches (85#)
4 X 5 Squats (165#)
4 X 5 Bench Press (135#)
Specialty Lifts
3 X 5 Bent arm flys (35#)
3 X 5 Incline Press (100#)

DAILY SEASONAL WORKOUTS
Fall
Volleyball, weight training when possible
Winter
Basketball, weight training when possible
Pre-season drills when possible
Towel drills
Shadow drills
Throwing drills isolating one action
Spring
Throwing workout

Shot Put	Discus
5 throws over the back	15 throws standing half circle
8 throws standstill	25 throws full circle

12 throws half circles
20 throws full circles

Monday—Stretch, jog ½-mile, throwing workout, weight training program

Tuesday—Stretch, jog ½-mile, throwing workout, 5 X 50 sprints

Wednesday—Stretch, jog ½-mile, throwing workout weight training workout

Thursday—Stretch, jog ½-mile, throwing workout

Friday—Competition

Saturday—Weight training program, stretch, jog ½-mile, throwing workout

Sunday—Rest

Summer

Jackie continues her spring workout pattern through the summer, but reduces her weight lifting two weeks before major meets.

Clint Johnson

CLINT JOHNSON   Shawnee Mission South High School

Born 12/6/61   Shawnee Mission, Kansas

6-4   198   Coaches Verlyn Schmidt & Scott Calder

COMPETITIVE HISTORY

The National Freshmen, Sophomore, and Junior Class discus record holder and National Junior Olympic Champion, Clint is well on his way to becoming one of the nation's top all-time, all-around weightmen. He first participated in track as a seventh grader and also competes in football and basketball.

BEST MARKS
206-9   69-1¼

AGE GROUP MARKS

Year	Age	Discus (2# 3.5 oz)	Discus (3# 9oz)	Discus (4# 6.4 oz)	Shot (8)	Shot (12)
1975	13	147-4½			40-3	
1976	14	178-2	145-7		52-0	42-4
1977	15	196-0	181-1	147-4½	68-1	52-2
1978	16		196-0	161-1		60-6½
1979	17		200-2	177-7		65-3½
1980	18	206-9		——		69-1¼

PREPARING FOR COMPETITION

"I visualize a good throw and concentrate on how I felt when my previous throws were good."

TRAINING COMMENTS
"The most important part of my training is weight lifting. I prefer the OBOL Discus because the weight is on the rim; it seems to be more stable."

WEIGHT TRAINING PROGRAM
Clint works out doing power cleans, jerks, bench presses, flys, squats, front squats and incline presses. He does repetitions in pyramid style, 6-4-3-2-1 or 8-6-4-2.

DAILY SEASONAL WORKOUTS
Fall
Football—limited weight training
Winter
Basketball—light weight training twice each week
Spring
Clint alternates schedules, depending upon upcoming competition
Schedule I—working through a meet
Monday—Throw 30-40 times, run 5-10 stadium steps, jog 1 mile
Tuesday—Weight training program—Heavy
Wednesday—Throw 30-40 times, run 5-10 stadium steps, jog 1 mile
Thursday—Weight training program—Heavy
Friday—Throw 5-10 times, jog 1 mile
Saturday—Competition
Sunday—Rest
Schedule II
Monday—Weight training program—Heavy
Tuesday—Throw 30-40 times
Wednesday—Weight training program
Thursday—Throw 5-10 times, jog 1 mile
Friday—Jog 1 mile
Saturday—Competition
Sunday—Rest
Summer
Clint continues his spring training schedule throughout the summer.

Dan Krueger

DAN KRUEGER   Bayside High School

Born 2/5/60   Virginia Beach, Virginia

6-2   260   Coach Len Greenwood

COMPETITIVE HISTORY

Dan began his track career when junior high coach Jim
Royster talked him into trying the shot and discus. During
the summer he caught the track bug, and by the time he
reached high school he had dropped baseball and wrestling to
concentrate on his throwing.

The hard work paid off, as Dan has established 24 meet
records, put himself 5th on the all-time indoor list and 11th
on the all-time outdoor list. Dan finished 3rd in the 1978
Golden West Invitational and was named to the *Track &
Field News* and Adidas All-America Teams.

BEST MARKS
68-5½   188-7

AGE GROUP MARKS

Year	Age	Shot	Discus
1974	14	47-0 (#8)	130-0 (#2)
1975	15	60-8 (#8)	166-0 (#2)
1976	16	61-0 (#12)	155-0 (#3-9)
1977	17	62-5	170-2
1978	18	68-5½	188-7

PREPARING FOR COMPETITION

"I try not to become too psyched, because when I do, I find I have the problem of pushing too hard. When I go totally relaxed, I have a better day. Also, warming up very thoroughly is important to me. I warm up until I have a good sweat running and then I remove my sweats according to when I throw."

TRAINING COMMENTS

"To me, the most important part of my training has been viewing films of my throws to pick out things I can't see when I'm throwing. I take the film and run it frame by frame to see what needs improvement. To prepare myself for a meet, I concentrate on the points of my throwing which are weak . . . I work on them as often as possible."

WEIGHT TRAINING PROGRAM

Monday	Wednesday
Bench Press 10 X 5	Bench Press 10 X 5

Incline Press 3 X 8 Incline Press 3 X 8
Flyes 3 X 8 Flyes 3 X 8
Military Press 3 X 8 Curls 4 X 10
Deltoit Raises 3 X 8 Tricep work
Situps between each set Situps between each set

Friday
Bench Press 10 X 5
Incline Press 3 X 8
Flys 3 X 8
Squats 4 X 8
Leg Curls 4 X 10
Leg Extensions 4 X 10
Calf Raises 5 X 20
Situps between each set

DAILY SEASONAL WORKOUT
Fall
    Football
Winter
    Monday—Weight lifting workout and running
    Tuesday—Throw and run
    Wednesday—Weight lifting workout and running
    Thursday—Throw and run
    Friday—Rest
    Saturday—Competition
    Sunday—Analyze previous meet
Spring
    Monday—Weight lifting workout
    Tuesday—Throw shot and discus
    Wednesday—Weight lifting workout and/or competition
    Thursday—Throw shot and discus
    Friday—Rest
    Saturday—Competition
    Sunday—Analyze previous day's meet
Summer
    "I usually lift all summer and try to enter any AAU or
other meets to keep in the swing of things."

COMMENTS
    Dan uses the spin technique and feels that it will be the
technique of the future.

Dana Olson

DANA OLSON   Westlake High School

Born 7/15/61   Austin, Texas

5-4 138   Coach Harry Lehwald

COMPETITIVE HISTORY

Texas State Champion and discus record holder, Dana first became involved in track as a ten-year-old sprinter. In high school, she began year round training for the throwing events and has added numerous championships and records, including National Junior Olympic medals, to her performance credentials.

BEST MARKS

159-0 (d)   49-11   133-2 (j)

AGE GROUP MARKS

Year	Age	Discus	Shot	Javelin
1976	14	131-11	40-¾	
1977	15	141-0	42-3	
1978	16	152-7	43-5¼	133-2
1979	17	159-0	49-11	

PREPARING FOR COMPETITION

"I just try to relax and concentrate on my form."

TRAINING COMMENTS

Dana feels that her excellent coaches, Dorothy

Doolittle, now at University of Missouri, and Harry Lehwald have been the biggest reason for her success. Their training program and film analysis have improved her technique and pushed her to dedication to her events.

WEIGHT TRAINING PROGRAM

"I have been using free weights for a year and a half. I do bench press, incline press, incline flys, pull-overs, tricep press, standing press, leg extension, leg curl, dead lift, and abdominal exercises. I usually work up to a maximum or a 'heavy' and then do 3 sets of 8-10 reps."

DAILY SEASONAL WORKOUTS
Fall
　　Monday—Weight training program, basketball, 1-mile fartlek

106

Tuesday—Weight training program, basketball
Wednesday—Weight training program, basketball
Thursday—Weight training program, basketball
Friday—Basketball, jog 1-mile
Saturday—Discus—12 standing throws, 36-48 full throws
        Discus—12 standing throws, 20 full throws
Sunday—Rest

Winter

Monday—Weight training program, basketball
Tuesday—Weight training program, basketball
Wednesday—Weight training program, basketball
Thursday—Weight training program, basketball
Friday—Basketball
Saturday—Basketball
Sunday—Throwing workout or form work

Spring

Monday—Weight training program, sprint work, throwing workout
Tuesday—Weight training program, sprint work, throwing workout
Wednesday—Weight training program, sprint work, throwing workout
Thursday—Weight training program, sprint work, throwing workout
Friday—Sprint work, throwing workout
Saturday—Competition
Sunday—Rest

Throwing workout consists of discus, 14 standing throws and 50 full and shot put, 12 standing throws and 20 full

Summer

Monday—Weight training program, throwing workout, 10 X 60 yard sprints
Tuesday—Weight training program, throwing workout, 1-2½-mile jog
Wednesday—Weight training program, throwing workout, 10 X 60 yard sprints
Thursday—Weight training program, throwing workout, 1-2½-mile jog
Friday—Throwing workout, 10 X 60 yard sprints
Saturday—Throwing workout, 1-2½-mile jog
Sunday—Throwing workout

Peter Pallozzi

PETER PALLOZZI

Classical High School

Born 6/1/60

Providence, Rhode Island

6-1   215

Coach Alfred Morro

COMPETITIVE HISTORY

Starting in track as a freshman, Peter worked year-round on the weight events to become a two-time Rhode Island shot put champion.

BEST MARKS

59-11¾ 160-4 (d)   182-4 (j)

AGE GROUP MARKS

Year	Age	Shot	Discus	Javelin
1975	15	45-6	––	––
1976	16	50-1½	––	170-9
1977	17	55-5	140-0	162-7
1978	18	59-11¾	160-4	182-4

PREPARING FOR COMPETITION

"I concentrate very hard, until I'm almost obsessed.

TRAINING COMMENTS

Peter works hard on basic technique until he has it down pat, then adds the power.

WEIGHT TRAINING PROGRAM

Peter lifts weights on a basic strength program through the

summer months only.

DAILY SEASONAL WORKOUTS
Fall, Winter, and Spring
Monday-Saturday—Work on technique every day, gradually adding power to the throws. Run sprints every day.
Summer
Peter works with weight lifting and running programs through the summer.

George Saah

GEORGE SAAH   Montgomery Blair High School

Born 2/28/61   Silver Springs, Maryland

6-3 245   Coach Jack Wofford

COMPETITIVE HISTORY
Maryland State record holder in the shot put, George has been named to All-Metropolitan, All-State, and All-American honors.

BEST MARKS
65-3 182-4

AGE GROUP MARKS

Year	Age	Shot	Discus
1977	15	56-2½	157-0
1978	16	61-9	168-5½
1979	17	65-3	182-4

PREPARING FOR COMPETITION
"I think of myself as the biggest and strongest guy around, and I get really aggressive with the shot by throwing it from hand to hand until it starts to feel light. I think about how badly it feels to be second."

TRAINING COMMENTS
George feels that a good combination of form and strength work is important for shot and discus success.

WEIGHT TRAINING PROGRAM

Saah works with free weights three days each week through the fall and winter seasons. Workouts consist of incline press, bench press, military press, and lat machine pull downs.

DAILY SEASONAL WORKOUTS

Fall

Monday—24-45 form throws, jog one mile, weight training program

Tuesday—20 form throws, 20 mid-distance throws, jog 1-mile

Wednesday—10 form throws, 10 mid-distance, 20 distance throws, 10 X 40 yd. sprints, weight training program

Thursday—10 form throws, 5 mid-distance, 10 distance 40 yd. sprints, jog ½ mile

Friday—20 form throws, 5 mid-distance, 10 distance throws, ½-mile jog, weight training program

Saturday—Jog ½-mile, 20 form throws, 20 mid-distance throws, jog ½-mile

Sunday—Rest

Winter

Monday—Form work and short sprints, weight training program

Tuesday—20 form throws, 20 mid-distance, 20 short sprints.

Wednesday—10 form throws, 20 mid-distance, 10 distance throws, ½-mile jog, weight training program

Thursday—10 form throws, 10 mid-distance, 25 distance throws, 10 sprints

Friday—10 form throws, 20 mid-distance, 5 distance throws, ½-mile jog, weight training program

Saturday—Competition, work on mistakes after meet

Sunday—Off

Spring

Monday—20 form throws with shot, 15 with discus, jog 1 mile

Tuesday—20 mid-distance throws in shot and discus, run sprints

Wednesday—20 form throws, 25 distance throws, work on discus form

Thursday—25 to 40 distance throws in discus and shot

Friday—Form work only

Saturday—Competition

Sunday—Rest

Summer

George works out to stay in shape over the summer, but does very little shot or discus work.

George Scribellito

GEORGE SCRIBELLITO   Toms River North High School

Born 7/28/59   Beachwood, New Jersey

6-3   232   Coaches Ken Nichols & Joe Lykes

COMPETITIVE HISTORY
George became involved with track in order to weight lift for football. In his four years of competition, he has won many county, conference, and State championships, as well as a 2nd place at the Penn Relays and Eastern States Championships.

BEST MARKS
61-0

AGE GROUP MARKS

Year	Age	Shot
1975	15	47-2
1976	16	56-1½
1977	17	60-3
1978	18	61-0

PREPARING FOR COMPETITION
"I do this by sitting at home the night before a meet, sitting in meditation, concentrating on my competition. I find it's totally relaxing."

113

TRAINING COMMENTS

Weight training and "throwing for perfection" are the most important parts of George's practice program.

WEIGHT TRAINING PROGRAM

George uses ¾-squats, incline press, military press, bench press, flys, deadlifts, and cleans, doing five sets of five, or eight sets of three. He goes for maximum weight every two weeks.

DAILY SEASONAL WORKOUTS
Fall
George plays football, but works out for track as well
Monday—Weight training program, run stadium steps
Tuesday—3-5 miles
Wednesday—Weight training program, run sprints
Thursday—3-5 miles
Friday—Weight training program
Saturday—Football game
Sunday—Rest

Winter
Monday—Weight training program, run sprints
Tuesday—20-30 throws, jog 1 mile
Wednesday—Weight training program, run stadium steps
Thursday—20-30 throws, play basketball
Friday—Stretch
Saturday—Competition
Sunday—Rest

Spring
Monday—Weight training program, run sprints
Tuesday—40-50 throws, jog 1 mile
Wednesday—Weight training program, run stadium steps
Thursday—30-40 throws, run sprints
Friday—Stretch, jog ½ mile
Saturday—Competition
Sunday—Rest

Summer
George lifts weights four days a week, with throwing workouts twice a week. He competes in A.A.U. track meets whenever possible.

Mike Shill

MIKE SHILL   East Valley High School

Born 10/16/61   Newman Lake, Washington

5-11   220   Coach Howard Dolphin

COMPETITIVE HISTORY

Mike began his track and field career in the Spokane area's strong junior high program. Influenced by college coaches and athletes, he received a solid background in fundamentals and has developed into one of the outstanding weightmen of Eastern Washington.

BEST MARKS

63-2   190-5 (j)   166-6 (d)

AGE GROUP MARKS

Year	Age	Shot	Discus	Javelin
1975	13	58-2 (#8)		
1976	14	53-6 (#12)	140-0	
1977	15	58-10	150-0	
1978	16	63-2	166-6	190-5
1979	17	62-8½		

PREPARING FOR COMPETITION

"Set myself a goal and try to reach it."

TRAINING COMMENTS

Mike says that working on quickness and on weight

training has been the most important parts of his training.

WEIGHT TRAINING PROGRAM
Mike uses a varied weight training program, changing workouts according to the season or day.

Fall and Early Winter
Bench Press (#235) 1 X 10, 1 X 7, 1 X 5

Winter and Spring

Workout #1
Bench Press 1 X 10, 1 X 7, 1 X 5
Power Cleans 1 X 10, 1 X 7, 1 X 5
Curls 1 X 10, 1 X 7, 1 X 5
Dips 1 X 10, 1 X 7, 1 X 5

Workout #2
Squats 1 X 10, 1 X 7, 1 X 5
Leg Press 1 X 10, 1 X 7, 1 X 5
Ramrack Hamstring Exercise 1 X 10, 1 X 7, 1 X 5

Workout #3
Bench Press 1 X 10, 1 X 7, 1 X 5, 1 X 3, 1 X 1
  (heavy weights)
Power Cleans 1 X 10, 1 X 7, 1 X 5
Curls 1 X 10, 1 X 7, 1 X 5
Dips 1 X 10, 1 X 7, 1 X 5

DAILY SEASONAL WORKOUTS
Fall
Football and weight training
Winter
Monday—Weight training program #1
Tuesday—Weight training program #2
Wednesday—Weight training program #3
Thursday—Weight training program #2
Friday—Weight training program #3
Saturday—Run 1-3 miles
Sunday—Rest

116

Jog 1-2 miles each day, work every day on technique with throws in the 45-foot range; take 10-15 hard puts every Monday and Wednesday

Spring

Mike uses the same lifting and throwing schedule as during the winter, adding 40's and agility drills to maintain quickness. He tapers off on the weight training 1-2 days before big meets.

Summer

During the summer, Mike lays off the weights to work on technique and quickness, throwing 20-25 hard puts every other day.

Elaine Sobansky

ELAINE SOBANSKY   Trinity High School

Born 12/16/61   Washington, Pennsylvania

6-0   180   Coach Gerald & Mary Chambers

COMPETITIVE HISTORY
Elaine tried out for the track team when fellow classmates encouraged her to. She stuck with it, became State shot put champion, a nationally-ranked prep putter, and was named to the *Track & Field News* All-America Team.

BEST MARKS
48-7¾ (#8)   45-7 (4k)   120-2

AGE GROUP MARKS

Year	Age	Shot #8	Shot 4k	Discus
1977	15	42-4		104-2
1978	16	48-7¾	45-7	120-2
1979	17	50-8½	46-8	
1980	18	50-10i	50-1¼	

PREPARING FOR COMPETITION
"I think about my form and how my position ends up in the circle. I always set a goal before each meet."

TRAINING COMMENTS
Elaine feels her daily workouts have been the most important parts of her training. She works hard on various

118

parts of the event: balance, concentration, glide, turn, extention and explosion. Sprint work helps increase speed and long and triple jump work is done to aid balance and agility.

WEIGHT TRAINING PROGRAM

During the off-season, Elaine worked with both free weights and a weightlifting machine, concentrating on high repetitions of light weight with all lifts done in sets of three.

DAILY SEASONAL WORKOUTS

Fall

Some light track and field work, work with pre-season basketball program

Winter

Basketball

Spring

Monday—Shot and discus technique work

Tuesday—Competition

Wednesday—Shot and discus technique work, sprint workout

Thursday—Light throwing, jumping workout

Friday—Competition

Saturday—Shot and discus technique work, sprint or jumping workout

Sunday—Rest

Summer

Elaine does some weight lifting over the summer, but works mostly on the shot put, participating in as many meets as possible.

Philip Wells

PHILIP J. WELLS

C.S. Molt High School

Born 12/3/60

Warren, Michigan

6-4 240

Coach Steve Johnson

COMPETITIVE HISTORY
Taught shot putting fundamentals by his older brother, Philip found he enjoyed it and so followed in his sibling's footsteps. Knee injuries forced him to give up football, but he used the time to concentrate on strength training.

BEST MARKS
61-6 157-1

AGE GROUP MARKS

Year	Age	Shot	Discus
1975	14	48-10 (8#)	——
1976	15	58-11	——
1977	16	53-10 (12#)	133-9
1978	17	59-6	145-6
1979	18	61-6	157-1

PREPARING FOR COMPETITION
"I do sprints, jumping jacks, and a casual bob up and down like a boxer does when he dances in the ring. As I'm doing this, I repeat 'I can do it and I'm going to win.' "

TRAINING COMMENTS
Philip feels that his weight training and repetitive

form-work are the most important part of his training.

WEIGHT TRAINING PROGRAM
Monday-Wednesday-Friday

Bench Press	5 X 4	Bentover rowing	3 X 5
Incline Press	4 X 5	Dumbbell Press	3 X 5
Flys	3 X 8	Curls	5 X 5
Lat Pulldowns	3 X 8	Tricep Extension	5 X 5

Tuesday-Thursday

Squats	5 X 5
Leg Extension	4 X 4
Leg Press	4 X 4

DAILY SEASONAL WORKOUTS
Fall
Weight training program every day
Winter and Spring
Monday—Weight training program

Tuesday—10 finger flips, 10 arm tosses, 20 body & leg reverse throws, 20-30 full form throws

Wednesday—Weight training program

Thursday—10 finger flips, 10 arm tosses, 20 body & leg reverse throws, 20-30 full form throws

Friday—Throwing practice, finger flips, arm tosses, full form throws with glide and reverse

Saturday—Weight training program

Sunday—Rest
Summer
Wells works out with his weight training program every day throughout the summer.

Doug Woolen

DOUG WOOLEN   Pullman High School

Born 1/29/60   Pullman, Washington

6-2   210   Coach Phil Lafer

COMPETITIVE HISTORY

Doug joined the track team as a seventh grader and began throwing the discus as a ninth grader. The Washington State Champion in 1977 and 1978, Doug was 3rd in the 1977 Junior Olympics and 6th in the 1978 Golden West Invitational.

BEST MARKS
190-5   56-0   10.5

AGE GROUP MARKS

Year	Age	Discus	Shot
1975	15	134-10	44-7
1976	16	150-0	50-9
1977	17	182-2	52-10
1978	18	190-5	56-0

PREPARING FOR COMPETITION

"I really enjoy throwing, so before a meet I like to lay off for 1 to 3 days. By the time the meet starts, I'm really eager to throw. I also like to go through discus throws in my head. I spend a lot of time thinking about throwing. I sometimes watch films of Olympic throwers to get the correct form in my mind."

TRAINING COMMENTS

Doug has worked hard on his technique to perfect his smoothness and balance in the ring. He feels this has been more important than his strength building program.

WEIGHT TRAINING PROGRAM

Doug lifts 3 days a week for one hour a day, stretching before, during and after each workout to maintain his flexibility. He classifies his lifting workouts on the basis of heavy, medium, and light lifting days.

HEAVY WEIGHT TRAINING DAY
Bench press 3 X 5, 2 X 3, 2 X 1
Squats 3 X 5, 2 X 3, 2 X 1
Flips 5 X 5
Curls 4 X 5

MEDIUM WEIGHT TRAINING DAY
Squats 4 X 5
Bench press 5 X 3
Flips 4 X 5
Curls 4 X 5

LIGHT WEIGHT TRAINING DAY
Bench press 3 X 5
Flips 3 X 5
Cleans 3 X 5

DAILY SEASONAL WORKOUTS
Fall
Football
Monday—Heavy weight training program
Wednesday—Heavy weight training program
Friday—Football game
Saturday—Heavy weight training program
Winter
Daily warmup: jog ½ to ¾ mile, stretch, 880 accelerations (run straights, jog curves), 5-10 40 yard sprints, jog ¼

mile.

Monday—Heavy weight training program
Tuesday—Throw indoors easy
Wednesday—Heavy weight training program
Thursday—Throw 15-30 times indoors
Friday—Light weight training program
Saturday—Throw 15-30 times indoors, work on drills
Sunday—Throw 15-30 times indoors, work on drills

Spring

Daily warmup: jog ½ to ¾ mile, stretch, 5-8 100's on grass, 5-8 hill climbs, stretch
Monday—20-50 throws
Tuesday—Medium weight training program
Wednesday—20-50 throws
Thursday—Light weight training program
Friday—Light throwing—less than 20 throws
Saturday—Competition
Sunday—Heavy weight training program

Summer

Doug continues his spring program and competes in some big invitational meets.

JAVELIN THROW

Gray Barrow

GRAY BARROW   University High School

Born 12/4/59   Baton Rouge, Louisiana

5-11 165   Coach Jimmy Gilbert

COMPETITIVE HISTORY
An all-round athlete at University High involved in all sports, Gray fell naturally into track. He picked up the javelin one day, threw it with "natural" form, and stuck with it as his major event.

Nineteen-seventy-eight was a banner year for Gray, as he was Golden West Invitational and Junior Olympic runner-up as well as International Prep Invitational Champion. He was named to the *Track and Field News* and Adidas All-America Teams.

BEST MARKS
231-1

AGE GROUP MARKS

Year	Age	Javelin
1975	15	172-11
1976	16	190-11
1977	17	222-2
1978	18	231-1

PREPARING FOR COMPETITION
"Complete Concentration!!" "Blackout all other things around you and just concentrate on your event."

TRAINING COMMENTS
Flexibility work has been an important part of Gray's training program. He feels that it is also important to keep your cardiovascular system in shape.

WEIGHT TRAINING PROGRAM
Being a three-sport man at University High, Gray had little time for a regular weight training program. He did lift during the summer months, concentrating on a basic power program.

DAILY SEASONAL WORKOUTS
Fall
Football
Winter
Basketball
Spring
Monday—Flexibility warmup, including situps and push ups, hurdle and sprint work (330's, 220's, 110's)
Tuesday—Flexibility, hurdle and sprint work, javelin technique work
Wednesday—Flexibility, hurdle and sprint work (330's, 220's, 110's)
Thursday—Flexibility, go over javelin approach
Friday—Competition
Saturday—Rest
Sunday—Rest
Summer
Gray uses the summer months to concentrate on his weight training program and does a lot of sprint work to improve the quickness that he feels is important to his javelin throwing.

Tracy Beckes

TRACY BECKES   Mount Vernon High School

Born 3/13/63   Mount Vernon, Washington

5-8   150   Coach Darrell Pearson

COMPETITIVE HISTORY
A newcomer to track and field, Tracy worked up to district and State medalist honors as well as a Junior Olympic fourth place in her first year of competition.

BEST MARKS
153-10

AGE GROUP MARKS

Year	Age	Javelin
1978	15	144-10
1979	16	153-10

PREPARING FOR COMPETITION
"I usually just go through the steps in my head every night before bed and a lot during the day of competition."

TRAINING COMMENTS
Tracy feels that her weight training program and excellent coaching have helped her to her success.

WEIGHT TRAINING PROGRAM
Tracy works out on a Universal machine and leg

extension machine everyday before school. A normal workout consists of three sets at each station, 12-15 repetitions per set.

DAILY SEASONAL WORKOUTS
Fall
Everyday—Run cross-country workout, then throw easily for 45 minutes, working on approach steps.
Winter
Basketball
Spring
Everyday—Weight training program every morning, followed by approach work without throwing. After school—Warm-up with stretching and 2-lap jog, followed by 2 laps of ¾ speed 220's, 50, 75, and 220 sprints. Stretch, throw easily for 30 minutes, work on approach, then short approach easy throws, long approach easy throws, finished off with two or three long approach hard throws. Beckes does not throw two days before or the day after competition.
Summer
Tracy tries to keep the same workouts through the summer.

Cindy Browning

CINDY BROWNING   White River High School

Born 3/12/61   Buckley, Washington

5-10   142   Coach Engstrom

COMPETITIVE HISTORY
Cindy went out for track as a freshman, experimenting with all of the throwing events. She finally settled on the javelin and became State division champion.

BEST MARKS
150-8

AGE GROUP MARKS

Year	Age	Javelin
1977	16	133-11
1978	17	150-8
1979	18	140-10

PREPARING FOR COMPETITION
"It is very important to stretch out all over ... be relaxed and concentrate. Shaking arms and wrists is one way to loosen up and relax."

TRAINING COMMENTS
Team companionship is very important to Cindy. "Getting to know your teammates and how much fun you can have learning together ... sportsmanship is very

important . . . coaches are great." During competition, Cindy concentrates on keeping a loose grip on the javelin and keeping the tip about ten inches above her head during her approach.

WEIGHT TRAINING PROGRAM
Cindy lifts weights five days each week through the spring season.

> Bench press 10 to 80 pounds
> Leg press 94 to 210 pounds
> each lift is done 10-50 repetitions

DAILY SEASONAL WORKOUTS
Fall
No training
Winter
Basketball
Spring
Everyday—Weight training program, stretching and light running, form work and throwing practice
Summer
Cindy continues to work on form and throwing through the summer.

131

Brian Cullinan

BRIAN CULLINAN   Kennett High School

Born 10/7/59   Conway, New Hampshire

5-11   175   Coaches Don Trimble & John Rist

COMPETITIVE HISTORY
Brian dropped baseball for track in junior high and began throwing the javelin. A 3rd place finish at the 1978 Golden West Invitational topped his high school career which included State, New England, and A.A.U. Junior Olympic victories.

BEST MARKS
222-5   152-10   6400 points

AGE GROUP MARKS

Year	Age	Javelin	Decathlon
1973	13	125-0	
1974	14	157-8	
1975	15	179-4	
1976	16	200-5	5290
1977	17	222-5	5963
1978	18	220-8	6400

PREPARING FOR COMPETITION
"Nothing special, just try to get psyched during the week of a big meet."

TRAINING COMMENTS

Technique work is most important to a beginning javelin thrower, states Brian, especially concentrating on keeping the javelin "in line" and throwing through the tip. Weight training has also been an important part of the overall training program at Kennett High.

WEIGHT TRAINING PROGRAM

Dead lift, Bench press, Bent arm pull overs, Squats, Military press, Cleans.

Brian does 3 sets of a weight that can only be done 8 repetitions on each of the lifts. When he can complete 12 repetitions he increases the weight and reduces to 8 repetitions.

DAILY SEASONAL WORKOUTS

Fall

Football

Winter

Monday—Weight training program

Tuesday—Throw 3½-pound ball into a net

Wednesday—Weight training program

Thursday—Throw 3½-pound ball into a net

Friday—Weight training program

Saturday—Throw 3½-pound ball into a net

Sunday—Rest

Spring

Monday—Windsprints, throw at 50% effort, work on technique

Tuesday—Competition

Wednesday—Technique work

Thursday—Competition

Friday—Short work on technique

Saturday—Competition

Sunday—Rest

Summer

Brian continues his winter weight training program through the summer.

ALL-AROUNDERS

Tonya Alston

TONYA LEE ALSTON   Chico Senior High School

Born 11/22/60   Chico, California

5-11 170   Coach Ms. Dale Edson

COMPETITIVE HISTORY

A national record holder in the 100 yard dash at age 9
(12.3), Tonya has continued to use her great natural talent to
achieve track and field success. Examiner Games and Junior
Olympic High Jump Championships add to a long list of
victories for this multi-talented athlete.

BEST MARKS

5-11½ 19-0 42-5(s) 130-1(d)
10.8(100) 13.7(110h) 3755(pent)

AGE GROUP MARKS

Year	Age	HJ	LJ	H	Pent
1975	15	5-6		14.7	
1976	16	5-8		14.1	
1977	17	5-10		14.0	
1978	18	5-10	19-0	13.7	3755
1979	19	5-11½	——	——	3538h

PREPARING FOR COMPETITION

"I have no special method of building my confidence; I
just be myself. I talk and socialize with my competition and

try to be calm while physically getting ready for my events. This helps me relax and therefore I execute my event better. Socializing also tells me what my competition is thinking and whether they're nervous."

TRAINING COMMENTS

"I feel the most important part of my training are my goals for the future. I work for meets ahead of time, reaching out for the maximum."

WEIGHT TRAINING PROGRAM

Tonya does not lift weights, but feels she has above average natural strength.

DAILY SEASONAL WORKOUTS

Fall
No workouts

Winter
Basketball

Tonya does no track workouts, but does participate in invitational indoor meets

Spring
Monday—Jog 2-3 miles

Tuesday—Jog 1-mile, stretch, work on high jump technique

Wednesday—Jog 1-mile, stretch, hurdle work, 16 X 220

Thursday—Jog 1-mile, stretch, shot and discus work

Friday—Jog 1-mile, stretch, 16 X 220, work on weak field event

Saturday—Rest

Sunday—Rest

Summer
Summer workouts were used to work specifically on one event each day

Darnell Johnson

DARNELL LOUIS JOHNSON   Highland Springs High School

Born 12/3/58   Highland Springs, Virginia

6-2 175   Coach Doug Hunt

COMPETITIVE HISTORY

Darnell, Virginia's most sought after football player of the 1978 season, turned to track in an effort to improve his football. His overall athletic ability has paid off, making him an outstanding five-event man for Highland Springs.

BEST MARKS
9.9 22.0 23-8¼ 6-7½ 45-7

AGE GROUP MARKS

Year	Age	LJ	HJ	TJ	100	200
1977	18	23-1	6-4	—	9.9	—
1978	19	23-8¼	6-7½	45-7	9.9	22.0

PREPARING FOR COMPETITION

Darnell used his warmup exercises: jumping jacks, leg stretches, 4-count benders, windmills, 880 jog, and event run through, as his preparation for meets.

TRAINING COMMENTS

"Running over distances has been the most important part of my training."

WEIGHT TRAINING PROGRAM
Darnell used an overall strength program in his weight training. He lifted only through the winter season, using near-maximum weights on all lifts.

DAILY SEASONAL WORKOUTS
Fall
Football
Winter
Monday—Weight training program, run 2-3 miles
Tuesday—Go through events, technique work
Wednesday—Weight training program, easy technique work
Thursday—Light technique work
Friday—Rest
Saturday—Competition
Sunday—Rest
Spring
Monday—3 X 330, 2 X 220, 2 X 110, 6 X 40, 2 X 440
Tuesday—Rest
Wednesday—Competition
Thursday—Light technique work
Friday—3 X 330, 2 X 220, 2 X 110, 6 X 40, 2 X 440
Saturday—Rest
Sunday—Rest
Summer
Darnell did some light running and football workouts through the summer.

Bill Kuntz

WILLIAM D. KUNTZ   Colonia Senior High School

Born 6/16/60   Colonia, New Jersey

6-4   190

COMPETITIVE HISTORY
Bill's older brothers had been track team members at Colonia and he joined the team to "follow the family tradition."

BEST MARKS
6-8½   15.2   21-6½   11-0

AGE GROUP MARKS

Year	Age	HJ	Vault	LJ	120HH
1975	14	4-6	——	15-0	——
1976	15	5-6	10-0	——	——
1977	16	6-5¾	11-0	17-0	19.0
1978	17	6-8¼	11-0	21-6½	15.2

PREPARING FOR COMPETITION
Kuntz has no special method of "psyching up" for meet competition.

TRAINING COMMENTS
Bill feels that his weight training program has been the most important part of his training. Also, he feels it has

helped him to coordinate his styles and approaches of the various events.

WEIGHT TRAINING PROGRAM

The New Jersey vaulter uses a great many exercises in his program: leg press, bench press, curls, reverse curls, rowing, lateral press, quadraceps machine, European jump squats, toe raisers, dead lift, situps, pullups, pushups, shoulder press.

DAILY SEASONAL WORKOUT
Fall
No workouts
Winter
Monday—Weight training program
Tuesday—High jump technique work
Wednesday—Weight training program
Thursday—Hurdle practice, high jump technique
Friday—Weight training program
Saturday—High jump work
Sunday—Rest
Spring
Monday—Weight training program
Tuesday—High jump technique work
Wednesday—Weight training program
Thursday—Technique work on all events, 120HH, HJ, PV, LJ
Friday—Weight training program
Saturday—High jump work
Sunday—Rest
Summer
Bill worked out with a running program along the New Jersey beaches and his regular weight training program.

Paul Lacassagne

PAUL LACASSAGNE   Chalmette High School

Born 5/19/61   Arabi, Louisiana

6-2 185   Coach Piazza

COMPETITIVE HISTORY
The Louisiana Indoor record holder and State Champion, Paul was asked to go out for track when Coach Piazza saw him stuff a basketball during freshman gym class.

BEST MARKS
6-9 21-4 42-6¼ 189-7(j)

AGE GROUP MARKS

Year	Age	HJ	LJ	TJ	Javelin
1978	16	6-5¾	20-0	39-3¼	162-6
1979	17	6-9	21-4	42-6¼	189-7

PREPARING FOR COMPETITION
"I like to just sit and talk to whomever is around because it keeps my mind off jumping and relaxes me. When it's my turn to get up and jump, I take a couple of deep breaths and approach the bar with confidence. Pressure of competition seems to psych me up."

TRAINING COMMENTS
Paul feels that playing basketball, because of the short

sprints and jumping, has helped his high jump ability. He uses a fast approach, concentrating on converting the speed into maximum height.

WEIGHT TRAINING PROGRAM

Leg Press and Squats
5 X 15   400#
Paul lifts a great deal for 3 months before the season, then decreases to 2 days each week. He also did leg exercises on a "hydro-lift" machine.

DAILY SEASONAL WORKOUTS
Fall and Winter
Monday—Weight training program
Tuesday—½-mile warm-up, 3 step jumps for form, ½-mile jog
Wednesday—Work on approach speed
Thursday—Weight training program
Friday—20 jumps for height
Saturday—Weight training program
Sunday—½-mile run
Spring
Monday—½-mile warm-up, work on approach speed, jump for form, ½-mile jog
Tuesday—Weight training program—increasing weight and repetitions from winter
Wednesday—Jumping drills; stuffing a basketball, standing jump onto a stack of 7-8 soda cases, landing on top without bending knees
Thursday—25 jumps for height
Friday—Weight training program
Saturday—1-mile run
Sunday—Light weight lifting work

Summer
Paul practices jumping twice a week, works with an overall weight training program and jumps in 1 AAU meet each week with the Mardi Gras Track Club.

142

Carol Lewis

CAROL LEWIS   Willingboro High School

Born 8/8/63   Willingboro, New Jersey

5-10   150   Coach Minore

COMPETITIVE HISTORY

Beginning as an 11-year-old Jesse Owens Games Champion, Carol has produced an impressive list of credentials in the past few years. She was State, Penn Relays, and National AAU Junior champion as a 14-year-old. Carol attended the Olympic Developmental Camp and was named to the *Track & Field News* All-American Team.

BEST MARKS
20-7¼   5-7½   13.7(h)   3,349(pent)

AGE GROUP MARKS

Year	Age	LJ	HJ	Hurdles	Pentathlon
1974	10	15-6	4-2	8.0	—
1975	11	16-8¾	4-8	7.6	—
1976	12	17-11½	5-2	12.1	—
1977	13	18-8¼	5-4	11.9	3,349
1978	14	20-5½	5-7	13.7	—
1979	15	20-7¼	—	—	—
1980	16	21-4½	—	—	—

PREPARING FOR COMPETITION
"I have to be in a good mood and be happy. When I'm in a good mood I like to move around, that's what gets my adrenaline flowing. I also like to talk a lot; it relaxes me before I jump."

TRAINING COMMENTS
"The most important part of my training is the people I train with. Training with a friend makes the atmosphere less tense. You relax more and get more out of your practice."

Carol uses an approach of 126'-130', varying the length depending upon track conditions, and feels that having a comfortable approach is the most important aspect of long jumping.

WEIGHT TRAINING PROGRAM
Lewis lifted weights two mornings each week, doing

144

upper body lifts once a week during gymnastics season.

Leg extensions	
Leg curls	
Grinder	40% max 3 sets of 20 repetitions
Lat pulls	
Bench press	
Cleans	60% max 1 set of 20 repetitions
Squats	

DAILY SEASONAL WORKOUTS
Fall
Gymnastics
Winter
Monday, Wednesday, Friday—Ladder workout (140, 280, 420, 560, 420, 280, 140)

Tuesday, Thursday—Long jump work consisting of bounding on a trampoline for knee lift, bounding on and off boxes of various heights, and jumping on two feet on and between boxes emphasizing lead leg and trail leg snap.
Spring
Monday—Wednesday—Long jump box drill (as in winter), 6 X 440 at ¼ speed, 6 X 220 at ½ speed, 6 X 100 at ¾ speed, 6 X 50 at full speed from blocks. A special long jump runway drill often replaces the 100's and 50's. Carol measures her approach on the runway, and works on running the 130's in exactly 5.0 seconds, concentrating on consistency. She runs 6 approaches every 3 minutes to duplicate competition situations, doing 5 sets of 6 approaches.

Tuesday—Thursday—Hurdle work, concentrating on lead leg and trail leg snap. Long jump form work and pop-ups. Carol jumps off an incline board to get extra emphasis on lift off the board and gaining extra height for practice of hitch-kick, hang and landing technique.
Summer
Carol continues her spring workouts through the summer season.

John McIntosh

JOHN C. McINTOSH   Stevenson High School

Born 2/19/61   Sterling Heights, Michigan

6-3   160   Coach T. Propst

COMPETITIVE HISTORY
John went out for track because he had nothing else to do. An all-county, league, and city performer, he won the Michigan State Championship and had a season average over 6-10.

BEST MARKS
7-0 21-6 14.8 40.1

AGE GROUP MARKS

Year	Age	HJ	LJ	HH	LJ
1974	13	4-10	16-9	——	——
1975	14	5-2	17-0	——	——
1976	15	5-10	17-4	18.7	——
1977	16	6-4	18-0	17.2	——
1978	17	6-10	20-3	15.1	42.0
1979	18	7-0	21-6	14.8	40.1

PREPARING FOR COMPETITION
"I'm not thinking about the other jumpers; my competition is the crossbar. If I think positively toward jumping my best and getting my jumps cleared on first

attempts, I don't feel too much more is worth worrying about; but I always enjoy a clean chart while jumping in meets."

TRAINING COMMENTS

"A weight training program is a must, and distance is as important." John, an outspoken athlete, feels that many jumpers overtrain. "Get at least one practice at the bar each week, making sure your approach is perfect. Go to as many big meets as possible and listen and watch other jumpers. The best way to improve in jumping is to get experience jumping and take advice carefully and experiment with it."

WEIGHT TRAINING PROGRAM

Squats	4 reps	200#
Bench Press	3 reps	175#
Curls	3 reps	75#
Rows	3 reps	75#

DAILY SEASONAL WORKOUTS
Fall and Winter
Monday—Weight training program
Tuesday—6-8 miles
Wednesday—Weight training program
Thursday—6-8 X 880
Friday—Weight training program
Saturday—8-10 miles
Spring
Monday—Weight training, squats & bench press only
Tuesday—Competition
Wednesday—Weight training, run 4 miles
Thursday—Competition
Friday—Weight training, run 4 miles
Saturday—Competition
Sunday—Rest
Summer
John works out just enough to keep in shape.

Steve Pace

STEVE PACE　　　　　　Spencerport Central High School

Born 5/6/61　　　　　　　　　Spencerport, New York

6-0　160　　　　　　Coaches Frank Greco and Paul Mroz

COMPETITIVE HISTORY
Steve began high jumping in his junior high track program. He has since become a New York State indoor champion.

BEST MARKS
6-10½　21-10½　44-10

AGE GROUP MARKS

Year	Age	HJ	LJ	TJ
1974	12	4-7	—	—
1975	13	5-4	—	—
1976	14	5-8	18-8	—
1977	15	6-5¼	19-2	38-2
1978	16	6-8¼	21-10½	42-5
1979	17	6-10½	21-1¾	44-10½

PREPARING FOR COMPETITION
"Before every jump, I talk myself into using the right form and good knee drive and not to worry about the height."

TRAINING COMMENTS
"The most important part of my training has been

148

weight training and technique. My ability to convert my horizontal speed into vertical lift is most important." Steve uses a 44-foot approach, 16-3 out from the standard.

WEIGHT TRAINING PROGRAM
Steve did all lifts, except squats, on a Universal machine.

Curls	2 X 20	90 pounds
Leg Press	2 X 10	500 pounds
Military Press	2 X 20	100 pounds
Toe Raises	1 X 10	390 pounds
Bench Press	2 X 10	140 pounds
Squats	1 X 10	350 pounds

Isometrics for quadriceps and hamstring strength.

DAILY SEASONAL WORKOUTS
Fall
Monday—1-mile warm-up, 6 miles at 6 minute/mile pace

Tuesday—1-mile warm-up, 6 miles in 1 mile intervals

Wednesday—10 miles

Thursday—1-mile warm-up, 6 miles at 6 minute/mile pace

Friday—1-mile warm-up, 6 miles in 1 mile intervals

Saturday—Cross Country Meet

Sunday—Rest

Winter
Monday—1-mile, weight training program, box drills, 2 miles

Tuesday—1-mile, approach work, bounding drills, 2 miles

Wednesday—1-mile, weight training program, box drills, 2 miles

Thursday—1-mile, 10 minutes stair running, 2 X 15 30 yard sprints, 2 miles

Friday—1-mile, approach work, 2 miles

Saturday—Competition

Sunday—Rest

Spring
Monday—1-mile, sprint workout, weight training program, 1 mile

Tuesday—Competition

Wednesday—1-mile, weight training program, box drills, 1 mile

Thursday—1-mile, sprint workout, bounding drills, approach work, 1-mile

Friday—Competition

Saturday—Rest

Sunday—Rest

Summer

Steve modifies his spring program, working out on his own to compete in summer meets.

Ken Riedl

KENNETH MARK RIEDL   Cheyenne Central High School

Born 10/25/59   Cheyenne, Wyoming

6-0   155   Coach Jim McLeod

COMPETITIVE HISTORY

Ken started running A.A.U. track as a third grader under his future high school coach McLeod. Watching the Olympics on television added to his track interests as he gave up football and basketball to concentrate on track.

Ken has had a great deal of success in Rocky Mountain area meets: Wyoming State hurdle champion, high-point man in the Wyoming Meet of Champions, and six-event winner in the 1978 Tri-State Invitational.

BEST MARKS

14.1   38.6   22-10½   47-7½   64

AGE GROUP MARKS

Year	Age	LJ	TJ	HJ	120HH
1973	13	16-6	36-0	4-10	——
1974	14	17-0	38-0	5-0	17.8
1975	15	18-6	39-6	5-4	16.5
1976	16	19-6	41-10	6-0	15.2
1977	17	21-11	44-4	6-2	14.4
1978	18	22-10½	47-7½	6-4	14.1

PREPARING FOR COMPETITION

"Just a lot of stretching, jumping drills and running. Just thinking about putting all I have into the jump and going through the full jump in my mind before I do it is the only 'psyching up' I do."

TRAINING COMMENTS

Ken feels that the amount of time spent on jumping technique and weight training has added the most to his performance. Working out on a "Leaper" machine, he feels, built up quite a bit of spring in his legs and working over boxes, hurdles, and bars, has aided his technique.

WEIGHT TRAINING PROGRAM

A "Leaper" machine was used every other day at 30reps/twice through. Ken also used a Universal weight machine, using 75% of maximum at each station, 3 times around the machine at 10 reps at each station.

DAILY SEASONAL WORKOUTS

Fall

Monday—Jog 2 miles, strides and stretch for 30 minutes, weight training program

Tuesday—Jumping over boxes & technique work, strides and bounding drills

Wednesday—Jog 2-4 miles, stretch, weight training program

Thursday—Work on jumping technique, strides

Friday—Jog 5 miles, stretch, weight training program

Saturday—Easy jog

Sunday—Easy jog

Winter

Monday—Jog 2-3 miles, strides and stretch, hurdle workout, weight training program, swim

Tuesday—Interval work (220's-330's), technique work on all events

Wednesday—Jog 2-4 miles, strides and stretch, event work, weight training program, swim

Thursday—Hard hurdle workout, work on jump approaches, interval work (220's-330's)

Friday—Jog easy, stretch and strides

Saturday—Competition

Sunday—Jog easy

Spring

Monday—Jog 2-3 miles, strides and stretch, weight training program, swim

Tuesday—Hard interval work (220's-330's), 1½ hours work on technique

Wednesday—Jog 4 miles, weight training program, strides, and stretch

Thursday—Work on event technique, strides, interval work (220's-330's)

Friday—Easy jog and stretch

Saturday—Competition

Sunday—Easy jog

Summer

"I run A.A.U. track and run about the same workouts, except not as much emphasis on the weight training; but the same workout a week is pretty regular, just like a spring week.

Anna Marie Solomonson

ANNA MARIE SOLOMONSON   Chinacum High School

Born 9/7/60   Chinacum, Washington

6-0   145   Coach Bob Flaherty

COMPETITIVE HISTORY

A volleyball and basketball player, Anna became interested in track, tried high jumping and liked it. A district champion and State runner-up in 1978, she also gained valuable international experience against the New Zealand National Team.

BEST MARKS

5-9   17-1

AGE GROUP MARKS

Year	Age	HJ	LJ	100
1976	15	5-0	15-0	13.8
1977	16	5-4	16-1½	13.3
1978	17	5-9	17-1	12.1

PREPARING FOR COMPETITION

Anna uses "visual synthesization, goal setting, and talks with her coach" before she competes.

TRAINING COMMENTS

Technique drills and weight training have been

important factors in Anna's training. She also feels that Coach Flaherty's leadership and work have helped her perfect her technique. Using a modified "J" approach, they have worked on a number of plans, making minor changes until the most successful was found.

During her jumping, Anna tries to concentrate on seven areas:
1. Consistency of approach
2. Leaning into the curve
3. Foot plant
4. Strong knee drive and arm lift
5. Driving hips up
6. Body arch over the top of the bar
7. The landing

WEIGHT TRAINING PROGRAM
Bench Press, Curls, Reverse Curls, Leg Press, Squats

"All lifts are done in sets of 3, repetitions are progressive to a pre-decided number depending on the lift. After the number of reps is easily reached, the weight is increased, reps decreased and then built up again.

DAILY SEASONAL WORKOUTS
Fall
Monday—Weight training program, sprints in gym
Tuesday—Off
Wednesday—Weight training program, 20 stairs X 6, running with 30 pound collar
Thursday—Off
Friday—Weight training program, sprints in gym
Saturday—Off
Sunday—Weight training program, sprints in gym, basketball
Winter
All workouts preceded by 15-20 minutes of stretching
Monday—Weight training program, 3 sets situps
Tuesday—Jumping drills (back jumping, triple jump drill, knee-arm drill)
Wednesday—Weight training program, situps

Thursday—Jumping drills

Friday—Weight training program

Saturday—Jumping Practice—work on approach and all other factors

Sunday—Weight training program, situps

Anna also played basketball throughout the winter season.

Spring

Monday—Weight training program

Tuesday—High jump/long jump technique work, sprint, relay practice

Wednesday—Weight training program

Thursday—High jump/long jump technique work, sprint, relay practice

Friday—Weight training program

Saturday—Competition or day off

Sunday—Weight training program

Summer

Anna continues her spring training program and participates in an A.A.U. program, often helping to work with younger athletes.

Carina Westover

CARINA WESTOVER

Born 7/5/61

5-11   132

Kiona-Benton High School

Benton City, Washington

Coach Doug Jeffries

COMPETITIVE HISTORY
A three sport athlete from a small school, Carina was State high jump and pentathlon champion and AAU Junior National runner-up.

BEST MARKS
5-11   17-1   11.1(80h)   25.9(220)   3568(pent)

AGE GROUP MARKS

Year	Age	HJ	LJ	HH	220	Pent
1975	13	5-2			27.8	
1976	14	5-4			26.9	
1977	15	5-6			25.9	
1978	16	5-11	17-4	11.1		3568
1979	17	5-10				3707a

PREPARING FOR COMPETITION
"I believe in myself and I'm confident as an athlete. Before I compete, I tell myself 'I can do it'. Also, I write letters to myself and read them just before competing. I may write these letters as much as a year in advance of a certain meet."

157

TRAINING COMMENTS

"Coach Jeffries pushes me physically," says Carina, "but also he helps me gain confidence and supports me; he's there when I need him." Carina concentrates on overall conditioning rather than on technique in her training.

WEIGHT TRAINING PROGRAM
No weight training

DAILY SEASONAL WORKOUTS
Fall
Volleyball
Winter
Gymnastics
Spring
Monday—1 X 110 (14.5 sec), 1 X 165 (22.3 sec), 1 X 220 (30.4 sec), 1 X 275 (39.7 sec)
Tuesday—1 X 275 (39.7 sec), 2 X 440 (72 sec), 1 X 660 (2:03 sec), work on approach and take off
Wednesday—1 X 110 (14.9 sec), 1 X 165 (22.9 sec), 2 X 220 (30.3 sec), 1 X 275 (40.8 sec), 12 sets of hurdles
Thursday—1 X 110 (14.5 sec), 1 X 165 (22.3 sec), 1 X 220 (30.4 sec), 1 X 275 (39.7 sec), work on bar clearance
Friday—2 X 110 (16.3 sec), 2 X 165 (25 sec), 2 X 220 (34.2 sec), 2 X 275 (44.7 sec), work on hurdle and high jump technique
Saturday—4-5 miles easy
Sunday—4-5 miles easy
Summer
No summer workouts.

Warren Wilhoite

WARREN WILHOITE   Winslow High School

Born 6/30/61   Winslow, Arizona

6-0 155   Coach Cranston Hysong

COMPETITIVE HISTORY

As a 4th grader Warren found he could run faster than anyone in his elementary school. Realizing his talent, he maintained an interest in track, as well as participating in other sports. A three-time All-State trackman, he has been one of the Southwest's top performers in the long jump and 440 for several years.

BEST MARKS

24-11   21.7   47.8   9.8

AGE GROUP MARKS

Year	Age	LJ	220	440	100
1974	12	16-9	—	—	—
1975	13	18-5	26.9	—	—
1976	14	20-4	23.3	53.8	11.3
1977	15	22-10½	23.0	50.4	10.8
1978	16	24-10½	22.0	48.5	10.0
1979	17	25-2¾	21.7	47.8	9.8

PREPARING FOR COMPETITION

"I usually set a goal in my mind at the beginning of the week . . . and keep telling myself that I will jump it."

TRAINING COMMENTS

"The most important part of my training has been the added strength I've gained through the year by running and weight lifting. When I was a freshman I used about a 55-foot approach because I'd become tired before getting to the end of the runway. Now my approach is 115 feet and I maintain speed all the way."

WEIGHT TRAINING PROGRAM

Full Squats	1 X 25, 2 X 15 (110#)
Arm Curls	1 X 15, 1 X 10, 1 X 8 (80#)
Leg Curls	1 X 25, 1 X 20, 1 X 15 (30#)
Leg Extensions	1 X 25, 1 X 20, 1 X 15 (30#)
Jump Squats	1 X 25, 2 X 15 (80#)

DAILY SEASONAL WORKOUTS

Fall

Football—running and weight training when time

Winter

Basketball—no indoor track in Arizona

Spring

Monday—2 X 550, 1 X 440, 2 X 220, 2 X 110, weight training program

Tuesday—6 X 110, long jump over boxes, run stairs

Wednesday—6 X 220, form work in long jump of boxes—20-40 pop-ups

Thursday—Starts, 3 X 20, 3 X 40, 3 X 60

Friday—Competition

Saturday—Competition

Sunday—2-6 mile run

Summer

Monday—6 X 330, 10 full run long jumps without boxes, weight training program

Tuesday—6 X 110 fast, weight training program

Wednesday—Starts at 20, 30, 40, 50, 60, 70, 80, 90 yards, light weight training

Thursday—Starts

Friday—Travel

Saturday—Competition

Sunday—Rest